Unlock Your
NATURAL GENIUS

With the Tools to Discover, Activate, and Thrive.

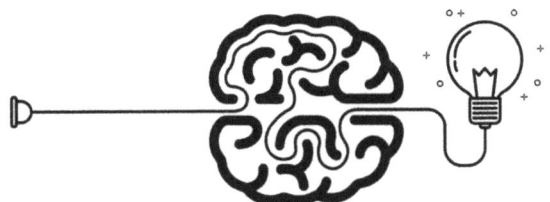

Dr. Jason E. Gines

Unlocking Your Natural Genius
Copyright © 2025 Dr. Jason E. Gines

Printed in the United States of America

Paperback ISBN: 978-1-965319-25-3

eBook ISBN: 978-1-965319-26-0

Purpose Publishing LLC.
13194 US Highway 301 South, Suite 417
Riverview, Florida 33578

www.PurposePublishing.com

Acknowledgments

First and foremost, I extend my deepest gratitude to my mother and father. Your unwavering example and the values you instilled in me, setting the tone, leading by example, and reaching beyond what's expected have shaped the foundation of my life and opened my world to possibilities I never imagined.

To my wife, my partner, my anchor, my heart, you have taught me the true meaning of patience and the profound depth of unconditional love. Your presence in my life is a living example of grace, and I am endlessly grateful.

To my four incredible children: you are my greatest teachers. Your honesty, curiosity, resilience, and love constantly remind me what it means to be fully human. Thank you for teaching me to grow, to listen, and to lead with compassion.

To my sister and brother, your unwavering support has held me up during life's most critical moments. You have been a source of strength when I needed it most.

Finally, to the countless students, colleagues, and friends who have held space for me, challenged me, and reflected back the genius I could not always see in myself, thank you. Your support and belief have been a mirror and a muse, and much of the inspiration for this book is rooted in those sacred connections. This work is as much yours as it is mine.

Your words might be the spark someone else needs to unlock their natural genius.

Dedication

To every soul who reminded me I had genius to unlock. You didn't just inspire this book. You are this book.

Table of Contents

Chapter 1
Understanding the Five Types of Genius 1

Chapter 2
The Power of Visionary Genius 21

Chapter 3
The Power of Relational Genius 37

Chapter 4
The Power of Execution Genius 51

Chapter 5
The Power of Creative Genius 65

Chapter 6
The Power of Physical Genius 79

Chapter 7
Time to Find Your Genius (Yes, You!) 93

About the author 112

Index 115

Appendix 118

Reference List 135

This page intentionally left blank

Chapter 1

Understanding the FIVE TYPES OF GENIUS

What If You Were Already a Genius?

What if you were already a genius, but no one ever told you? What if your brilliance wasn't measured by a standardized test, a GPA, or how well you memorized facts but by something deeper, something uniquely yours? For many, the idea of being a genius feels like a far-off dream reserved for the Einsteins and Mozarts of the world. However, the truth is that "genius" isn't exclusive to a select few. It exists in all of us in different ways. Unfortunately, however, we've been conditioned to believe that intelligence and success follow a singular, predefined path.

The Early Signs of Genius

Think back to when you were a child. What were you naturally drawn to? Maybe you spent hours drawing intricate pictures, piecing together model airplanes, or telling elaborate stories. Perhaps you had a knack for making people laugh or instinctively knew how to lead a group of friends. As children, we follow our instincts. We don't overthink what excites us, we just do it. However, those natural inclinations get buried under expectations somewhere along the way.

Parents, teachers, and society often reward certain types of intelligence while overlooking others. If you were good at math or science, you were labeled "smart." If you excelled in sports, you were seen as "talented." However, if your skills didn't fit into one of these accepted categories, and your genius showed up in ways that weren't easy to measure, it may have gone unnoticed or undervalued. In reality, intelligence and talent manifest in many different forms, but not all of them get the recognition they deserve.

How Society Defines Intelligence

Our world tends to reward a narrow definition of intelligence that prioritizes academics, logic, and measurable skills. Schools emphasize test scores, IQ levels, and structured learning, creating the illusion that intelligence can be ranked and compared. However, intelligence is far more dynamic. It's not just about what you can memorize or how well you perform on standardized tests.

Consider the way we celebrate traditional intelligence. Society highlights individuals with exceptional mathematical, scientific, or literary abilities, calling them "geniuses." However, what about the person who intuitively knows how to fix anything with their hands? What about someone who can walk into a room and instantly lift the energy, making everyone feel seen and valued? Or the person who can simplify and turn a complex idea into a compelling story? These abilities may not always be recognized in a classroom, but they are just as important, and in many cases, they are the true indicators of genius.

Howard Gardner, a renowned psychologist, introduced the theory of multiple intelligences, arguing that intelligence isn't a single measurable entity but rather a spectrum of different abilities. He identified areas like spatial intelligence (thinking in pictures), kinesthetic intelligence (learning through movement), and interpersonal intelligence (understanding and connecting with people) as equally valuable forms of intelligence (Gardner, 1983; 1993). This means that if you struggled in school, it wasn't because you weren't smart; it's because the system wasn't designed to measure your kind of genius.

Have You Been Looking in the Wrong Places?

Perhaps you've gone through life thinking you're "not smart enough" because you struggled with math or you weren't a straight-A student. Maybe you felt out of place because your interests didn't align with traditional academic success. That said, what if you were looking in the wrong places?

Think about the skills and talents that come naturally to you. Do you have an uncanny ability to bring people together? Can you fix anything with your hands, no matter how complex? Do you instinctively know how to comfort and guide others during difficult times? These are all forms of genius, but they often go unnoticed because they don't have a formal title or a structured grading system.

Take, for example, the case of Richard Branson, the billionaire founder of the Virgin Group. Branson struggled in school due to dyslexia and was often seen as a below-average student. Rather than letting that define his intelligence, he leaned into his strengths: visionary thinking, risk-taking, and people skills. His ability to connect with others, see opportunities where others didn't, and embrace unconventional thinking led him to become one of the most successful entrepreneurs in the world. His story proves that intelligence isn't about fitting into a system; it's about discovering how your mind works best and using that to your advantage (Branson, 1998).

Genius Is About Alignment, Not Just Intellect

The truth is that genius isn't just about intellect, it's about alignment. It's about recognizing and harnessing your natural strengths, passions, and aptitudes in a way that allows you to thrive. When you align your life with your genius, everything changes. You no longer feel like you're forcing yourself to fit into a mold never meant for you. Instead, you begin to operate with ease, confidence, and fulfillment.

For instance, consider a chef who never excelled academically but has an innate understanding of flavors, textures, and presentation. They don't just follow recipes; they innovate, creating dishes that tell a story. Now, think about a firefighter with an incredible ability to stay calm under pressure, assess dangerous situations with precision, and save lives. These individuals may not have been at the top of their class in traditional subjects, but they are undeniably geniuses in their own right.

The difference between those who embrace their genius and those who don't isn't intelligence, it's awareness. Many people go through life without ever realizing where their genius lies because they're too busy trying to measure themselves against the wrong standards. They spend years working in jobs that drain them, pursuing paths that don't align with their natural abilities, and wondering why they feel unfulfilled. Everything starts changing once you shift your perspective and recognize your unique genius.

Your Genius Already Exists, You Only Have to Claim It

So, what if your genius isn't in numbers or words but in relationships? What if your greatest strength isn't in solving equations but in solving conflicts? What if your gift isn't memorizing facts but creating beauty through art, movement, or music? The reality is your genius already exists. The question is whether you're ready to claim it.

Think about the moments in your life when you've felt completely in your element. What were you doing? Were you leading a group, fixing something, designing, teaching, or creating? These moments hold clues to your genius. Recognizing and embracing your unique strengths opens the door to a life of greater fulfillment and purpose.

The world needs all kinds of intelligence, visionaries, problem-solvers, artists, builders, healers, and leaders. Your genius, no matter what form it takes, is valuable. The sooner you start embracing it, the sooner you can begin making the impact you were destined to make.

In the chapters, we will explore the five types of natural genius, Visionary, Relational, Execution, Creative, and Physical, and help you uncover which one (or more) resonates most with you. By the end of this journey, you'll not only understand your own genius, but you'll also have the tools to use it in a way that transforms your life.

Breaking Free from the Old Definition of Genius

For centuries, intelligence was defined in narrow, rigid terms, measured by how well people could analyze, calculate, and recall information. Schools, IQ tests, and standardized exams reinforced the idea that intelligence was about academic performance. If you excelled at solving equations, memorizing historical dates, or writing grammatically flawless essays, people labeled you "smart." However, if you struggled with these tasks, society often labeled you as less capable, less intelligent, or even destined for mediocrity. This outdated definition has shaped how people think about their potential for generations, leaving many to believe they weren't born with the gifts necessary to achieve greatness.

Nonetheless, history proves otherwise. Some of the most successful and impactful figures of all time didn't fit this mold. They weren't necessarily the top students, the ones with perfect scores, or those who followed conventional paths to success. Instead, they were individuals who unlocked and harnessed their unique genius in ways that transcended traditional measures of intelligence.

Take Albert Einstein, for example. Today, his name is synonymous with genius, yet he struggled in school as a child. He had difficulty with rote memorization, often ignored classroom rules, and was even thought to have a learning disability. His teachers saw him as slow, not brilliant. What they failed to recognize was that Einstein thought differently. He had an extraordinary ability to visualize complex problems in his mind, something that traditional schooling never tested. Rather than conforming to a rigid academic system, Einstein leaned into his unique way of thinking, eventually developing groundbreaking theories that revolutionized physics. His genius was never about following the rules. It was about breaking them and reimagining how the world worked (Isaacson, 2007).

Maya Angelou, one of the most influential literary voices of the 20th century, also defied conventional definitions of intelligence. As a child, she faced immense trauma and self-doubt, even becoming mute for nearly five years (Angelou, 1969). A school system focused solely on grades and tests might have dismissed her as unremarkable. However, Angelou's genius wasn't in test scores. It was her ability to observe, feel passionately, and translate human experiences into words that resonated across generations. Through poetry, storytelling, and activism, she shaped American literature and culture, proving that genius can take the form of emotional depth, wisdom, and the power to connect with others through language.

Then there's Michael Jordan, widely regarded as the greatest basketball player ever. Most people know the famous story of how he was cut from his high school basketball team, a moment that could have shattered his confidence. If intelligence and ability were determined strictly by early success, Jordan might have accepted defeat. Instead, he used that setback as fuel. His genius wasn't just about raw talent. It was about an unmatched work ethic, an ability to analyze his weaknesses, and a relentless drive to improve. His discipline and continual refinement of his craft over time cemented his status as an icon. His story teaches us that genius isn't just about being naturally gifted; it's about perseverance, adaptability, and the willingness to keep pushing forward despite failures (Lazenby, 2014).

Oprah Winfrey, too, faced rejection before finding her genius. She was fired from one of her first television jobs because producers claimed she wasn't a good fit for TV (Kelley, 2010). Had she accepted this judgment, she might have faded into obscurity, believing she wasn't talented enough. However, Oprah had a gift: an unparalleled ability to connect with people, tell stories, and inspire. Instead of abandoning her path, she leaned into her strengths, eventually building a media empire that has influenced millions. Her story demonstrates that genius isn't always recognized immediately by others. Sometimes, the world tells you that you don't have what it takes until you prove it wrong.

These stories reveal that genius isn't something external, something granted only to the lucky few who happen to excel in school. It's not just about intelligence in the traditional sense. True genius is about discovering and embracing what makes you exceptional. It's about leaning into your natural strengths rather than trying to force yourself into a predefined mold of success.

The problem with the old definition of genius is that it leaves so many people behind. It tells the artist that their creativity doesn't matter as much as math skills. It tells the empathetic, relationship-driven person that their ability to connect with others isn't as valuable as logical reasoning. It tells the hands-on problem solver that their mechanical instincts are less impressive than the ability to memorize facts. These limiting beliefs prevent people from recognizing their unique genius and keep them stuck in a cycle of self-doubt.

Let's imagine what would happen if everyone began to see their own abilities through a different lens. What if intelligence wasn't just about knowledge but about how you apply your strengths in a way that makes a difference? What if success wasn't about fitting into a rigid academic structure but aligning your talents with what truly fulfills you?

The truth is that genius comes in many forms. Some people are visionaries, able to see opportunities and solutions, whereas others see obstacles. Some are Relational Geniuses who are gifted in understanding emotions, resolving conflicts, and bringing people together. Others excel in execution, thriving in structure, organization, and efficiency. Some are creative. They're able to translate emotions into art, music, or storytelling. Many individuals are Physical Geniuses, mastering movement, coordination, and hands-on craftsmanship.

Each of these forms of genius is valuable. Each has the power to make a lasting impact. However, the first step is recognizing it within yourself. Einstein, Angelou, Jordan, and Winfrey became legends because they found a way to cultivate their unique gifts. They didn't wait for someone else to validate their intelligence or tell them they were geniuses. They claimed it for themselves.

So, here is the question: Will you do the same? Will you break free from the old definition of genius and start embracing what makes you extraordinary? The world is waiting for the unique strengths only you can bring. It's time to discover, nurture, and own your genius.

The Five Types of Natural Genius

We all have a natural way of thinking, creating, and contributing to the world. Because most people learn to focus on traditional forms of intelligence, such as academic achievement, test scores, and memorization, they rarely explore or cultivate their unique genius. This narrow definition of intelligence leaves many feeling inadequate or uninspired, believing they lack the brilliance others seem to have. The truth is that intelligence is not limited to what can be measured by exams or grades. It is far more expansive, deeply personal, and highly diverse.

In this book, we'll explore five types of natural genius that shape how you interact with the world. You may strongly identify with one or have a mix of multiple types. No single type is superior to another. They all serve different purposes and bring distinct value to society. By understanding your genius, you can break free from self-doubt, lean into your strengths, and create a fulfilling life aligned with who you authentically are.

1. Visionary Genius

"Visionary Genius" is the ability to see the bigger picture, innovate, and create long-term strategies. Those with this form of genius are natural forward-thinkers who don't just accept the world as it is, they imagine how it could be better. They are driven by possibilities, often spotting opportunities and connections others overlook. Visionary Geniuses can see past current limitations and think beyond the present moment, making them excellent at predicting trends, solving complex problems, and pioneering new ideas.

For example, a tech entrepreneur with Visionary Genius might look at the healthcare industry and imagine a future where artificial intelligence revolutionizes diagnostics, making medical care more precise and accessible. While others see the system as it is, the visionary sees what it could be. Similarly, a teacher with Visionary Genius might completely reimagine how students engage with learning, transforming a traditional classroom into a dynamic, interactive space where education becomes a journey of curiosity rather than a rigid structure. These individuals thrive on innovation and creativity, often pushing boundaries to make their ideas a reality.

However, visionaries can sometimes struggle with execution. Their minds are filled with big ideas, but without proper support, they may find it challenging to bring those ideas to life. Therefore, surrounding themselves with people who can help refine and implement their vision is key to their success.

2. Relational Genius

"Relational Genius" is the ability to connect sincerely with people, build strong relationships, and inspire others. Those with this form of genius excel in emotional intelligence, making them naturally  empathetic and perceptive. They understand people on an intuitive level, often sensing emotions and unspoken needs. Relational Geniuses are not just great at socializing; they genuinely care about others, making them effective leaders, mentors, and healers.

A social worker with Relational Genius, for example, may walk into a room and immediately sense the emotional state of a struggling client. Instead of relying solely on surface-level conversations, they understand what's happening beneath the words and can respond with enduring compassion and insight. Likewise, a leader with Relational Genius doesn't just manage a team. They cultivate a supportive and inspiring environment where individuals feel seen, valued, and motivated to do their best work. They understand the strengths and weaknesses of their team members and know exactly how to encourage and uplift them.

Relational Genius plays a vital role in building trust and fostering meaningful connections. However, those who possess this genius sometimes struggle with emotional boundaries. They can become intensely invested in the well-being of others, which may lead to burnout if they don't practice self-care. Learning how to balance emotional involvement with personal well-being is crucial for those with this gift.

3. Execution Genius

"Execution Genius" is the ability to take ideas and turn them into reality with precision and efficiency. While visionaries dream up possibilities, Execution Geniuses are the ones who ensure that things actually  get done. They thrive in structured environments, excel at organization, and have a remarkable ability to transform abstract concepts into tangible results. These individuals are highly dependable, detail-oriented, and disciplined, making them the backbone of any successful operation.

For instance, a project manager with Execution Genius might take a vague idea presented by a visionary leader and break it down into actionable steps, creating a timeline and ensuring every milestone is met on time. Without them, many great ideas would remain just that, ideas. Similarly, a chef running a high-paced kitchen must execute each dish flawlessly, maintaining quality and consistency while managing time-sensitive tasks under pressure.

Those with Execution Genius bring order to chaos and thrive on productivity. However, they can sometimes become so focused on efficiency that they overlook creativity or flexibility. While their ability to follow through is unmatched, learning to embrace adaptability and innovation can help them reach new levels of success.

4. Creative Genius

"Creative Genius" is the ability to express ideas beautifully through art, music, storytelling, and design. While all types of genius involve creativity in some form, this type emphasizes using  artistic expression to inspire, communicate, and evoke emotion. Those with Creative Genius have a unique way of seeing the world, often finding beauty and meaning in places others overlook. They are drawn to self-expression and have an innate ability to create something out of nothing.

For example, a filmmaker with Creative Genius doesn't just tell a story; they craft an experience that moves people on an emotional level. They have a talent for shaping narratives that resonate deeply, challenging perspectives, and leaving lasting impressions. Similarly, a musician with Creative Genius intuitively composes melodies that speak to the soul, using sound as a language of its own.

One challenge Creative Geniuses face is self-doubt. Because artistic expression is emotionally personal, they may fear rejection or feel their work isn't "good enough."

However, when they embrace their unique perspective and trust their creative instincts, they have the power to transform the world through their art.

5. Physical Genius

"Physical Genius" is the ability to master body intelligence, coordination, and craftsmanship. While many people associate intelligence with the mind, this form of genius proves that intelligence also lives in the body. Those with Physical Genius are acutely aware of movement, space, and physical mechanics. They learn best through action, excelling in areas that require precision, rhythm, and hands-on problem-solving.

For instance, a dancer with Physical Genius moves with effortless grace, turning their body into an instrument of artistic expression. Their innate sense of rhythm and movement allows them to captivate audiences through sheer physical mastery. Similarly, a mechanic with Physical Genius might instinctively know how to fix an engine just by listening to the sound it makes. They don't rely strictly on technical manuals. They *feel* and *understand* how machines work on a level that others can't quite grasp.

Traditional education systems prioritize intellectual and analytical abilities over physical intelligence and often overlook this type of genius. As a result, many individuals with Physical Genius may not realize the full extent of their capabilities. Recognizing and honing this talent can lead to mastery in athletics, craftsmanship, performing arts, and various technical trades.

Owning Your Genius

You can begin tapping into your full potential when you understand where your genius lies. Instead of forcing yourself into roles or paths that don't align with your natural strengths, you can embrace what comes naturally to you. Each type of genius offers a unique way of contributing to the world, and there is no one path to success.

By identifying and cultivating your genius, you can shift from a life of frustration and uncertainty to a life filled with confidence and purpose. This book's goal is to help you recognize, develop, and fully own your genius so that you can live a life that feels wholeheartedly aligned with who you are supposed to be.

What Happens When You Unlock Your Genius?

When you begin to operate in alignment with your natural genius, something powerful happens. Life no longer feels like an uphill battle. Instead, things flow effortlessly because you're working with your strengths rather than against them. Regardless, recognizing and embracing their genius isn't easy for many people. They've been conditioned to believe that intelligence or talent must look a certain way, that success must follow a predefined path, or that they are somehow not "good enough" to claim their genius. If you've ever felt this way, you're not alone. The good news? You don't have to stay stuck.

By learning to overcome common barriers, you can confidently step into your unique genius, stop comparing yourself to others, and create a life filled with joy, fulfillment, and impact. One of the first transformations that happens when you begin to own your genius is increased confidence. Instead of doubting yourself, you start recognizing your unique strengths. Many people struggle with self-doubt when it comes to realizing their own genius. They think, *Who am I to call myself gifted? Or what if I fail?* This mindset keeps them from stepping into their full potential. One of the biggest roadblocks to confidence is the belief that your skills or talents don't measure up to those of others. Maybe you love writing, but you don't feel like a "real" writer because you haven't published a book. Perhaps you have a talent for fixing things, but you think *I'm just handy, not a genius.* The truth is, your genius doesn't need external validation to be real. It exists because it is part of you. No one started as an expert; every great artist, leader, athlete, or entrepreneur had to step into their genius before the world recognized it. Consider J.K. Rowling, who doubted herself so much that she almost didn't submit *Harry Potter* to publishers (Smith 2013). She was rejected twelve times before finally landing a deal. Imagine if she had let those doubts stop her!

Another major breakthrough happens when you stop comparing yourself to others. You no longer feel the need to fit into someone else's mold of success. One of the biggest obstacles to stepping into your genius is the tendency to compare yourself to others. You might think *I'm not as good a leader as my boss. I don't have the creative mind of a designer. I can't speak as well as a great communicator.* Comparison makes us feel small and inadequate, causing us to abandon our path in favor of trying to fit someone else's mold. Instead of measuring yourself against others, focus on what makes you unique. Your genius isn't meant to look like anyone else's. It's intended to be entirely your own.

Think about Oprah Winfrey and Ellen DeGeneres, both incredibly successful talk show hosts, yet with distinctly different styles. Oprah brings philosophical, emotional storytelling, while Ellen thrives on humor and lightheartedness. If Ellen had tried to be Oprah, or vice versa, neither would have fully tapped into their genius. The next time you compare yourself to someone else, remind yourself this: My genius is mine alone. I don't need to be like anyone else. I only need to be the best version of myself.

Perhaps the most significant shift happens when you begin experiencing more joy and fulfillment. Work, hobbies, and relationships feel more meaningful because they align with your natural abilities. Many people feel stuck and unfulfilled in their careers or daily lives because they aren't working in alignment with their natural genius. Do you ever feel like you're forcing yourself to be good at something that doesn't come naturally? Maybe you're naturally creative, but your job demands rigid analytical thinking. Perhaps you love working with your hands, but you've been pushed into a desk job.

Life becomes exhausting when we work against our genius rather than with it. Even if you're in a job or situation that doesn't fully align with your genius, there are ways to infuse more of what you love into your daily life. Imagine you're a Relational Genius, but you work in a role that lacks human connection. Rather than feeling stuck, look for ways to leverage your gift, mentor a colleague, spearhead team-building activities, or switch to a role where your relational strengths are valued.

Finally, once you step into your genius, you begin to create impact effortlessly. When you work within your genius, you bring immense value to the world. Many people dismiss their own genius because they assume it's not valuable enough. They think *I'm just good at organizing things, that's not special,* or *I love telling stories, but that's not a real talent.* Your genius doesn't have to be world-changing to be meaningful. The things you do effortlessly and the strengths that come naturally to you are things that others struggle with. When you step fully into your genius, you impact people in ways you may not even realize. Think about Mr. Rogers, who merely used his ability to connect with children to create a legacy of kindness that impacted millions. His genius wasn't flashy but simply his ability to make people feel seen, valued, and loved (King, 2018).

The moment you stop doubting your genius, comparing yourself to others, or dismissing your strengths, your life begins to shift. You'll step into confidence, knowing you have something valuable to offer. You'll experience more joy and ease because you're operating in alignment with who you truly are. You'll make a greater impact, not by forcing yourself into someone else's mold, but by fully embracing your own. Your genius is already inside you. The only question is, are you ready to own it?

Imagine a world where people genuinely embraced their genius instead of trying to fit into a box they weren't designed for.

- ► The artist wouldn't feel pressure to become an accountant.

- ► The hands-on builder wouldn't be told that college is the only path to success.

- ► The empathetic listener wouldn't be forced into a technical job that drains them.

Instead, people would lean into their strengths, thrive in their passions, and make a difference in deeply fulfilling ways.

Your Genius Is Already Inside You

You don't have to be a world-famous innovator, a best-selling author, or a record-breaking athlete to be a genius. Your genius is already inside you. It's just waiting to be recognized and nurtured. In the next chapter, we'll explore our first area of natural brilliance: Visionary Genius. *Because once you truly own your genius, everything in your life starts to change.*

Chapter References

Angelou, Maya. *I Know Why the Caged Bird Sings.* Random House, 1969.

Branson, Richard. *Losing My Virginity: How I Survived, Had Fun, and Made a Fortune Doing Business My Way.* Crown Publishing, 1998.

Gardner, Howard. *Frames of Mind: The Theory of Multiple Intelligences.*
Basic Books, 1983.

Gardner, Howard. *Multiple Intelligences: The Theory in Practice. Basic Books*, 1993.

Isaacson, Walter. *Einstein: His Life and Universe.* Simon & Schuster, 2007.

Kelley, Kitty. *Oprah: A Biography.* Crown Archetype, 2010.

King, Maxwell L. *The Good Neighbor: The Life and Work of Fred Rogers.*
Abrams Press, 2018.

Lazenby, Roland. *Michael Jordan: The Life. Little*, Brown and Company, 2014.

Smith, Sean. *J.K. Rowling: A Biography–The Genius Behind Harry Potter.* Greenwood, 2013.

Chapter 2

The Power of VISIONARY GENIUS

Defining Visionary Genius

Visionary Geniuses possess a rare ability to transcend the present and foresee the future, blending innovative thinking with strategic foresight. Their talent lies in identifying emerging trends, predicting challenges, and connecting diverse ideas into groundbreaking solutions. Equipped with a future-oriented mindset, they pioneer new systems, products, and industries, reshaping how society operates. This innate capacity often manifests early in life, with individuals demonstrating curiosity and a knack for seeing patterns others miss. For example, a young entrepreneur might notice inefficiencies in everyday processes and imagine solutions that could transform entire industries. A research scientist might connect discoveries across different fields, leading to breakthroughs that revolutionize healthcare or technology.

This type of genius isn't confined to those in high-profile careers. It can be found in educators who envision new ways of teaching, community leaders who imagine more inclusive societies, and artists who challenge societal norms through their work. Consider Maya Angelou, whose literary contributions and activism reshaped perspectives on race, identity, and human rights. Her ability to articulate complex social issues in relatable terms exemplifies the essence of Visionary Genius. Similarly, Steve Jobs transformed technology not only by creating innovative products but also by envisioning how these tools could enhance human creativity and connectivity (Isaacson 2011).

Visionary thinking often begins with a keen sense of *curiosity*, a desire to explore what lies beyond the status quo. This curiosity leads to the discovery of patterns and connections that others overlook. For instance, Wangari Maathai's environmental work in Africa began with her recognition of the interconnectedness of deforestation, poverty, and social instability. By planting trees, she restored the environment while empowering local communities, illustrating how visionary solutions can address multiple challenges simul-taneously (Maathai 2006).

Moreover, Visionary Geniuses are driven by a passion for creating a better future. They are not content with incremental improvements. Instead, they aim to fundamentally reshape the systems and structures that shape our lives. This often requires taking bold risks and persevering through setbacks. Malala Yousafzai's advocacy for girls' education is a testament to the resilience and determination that characterizes visionary leaders. Despite facing life-threatening opposition, she has continued championing education as a means of empowerment and social progress (Yousafzai & Lamb 2013).

The ability to communicate one's vision is another crucial aspect of Visionary Genius. Ideas, no matter how innovative, must be shared in ways that inspire and mobilize others. Oprah Winfrey's success lies in both her media ventures and her ability to connect with diverse audiences on a deeply personal level (Kelley 2010). Through her storytelling, she has fostered empathy, challenged societal prejudices, and encouraged individuals to pursue their dreams.

Visionary Genius is defined by the capacity to envision a more innovative, sustainable, and inclusive future. It involves recognizing patterns, imagining new possibilities, and inspiring others to join in the pursuit of that vision. Whether in technology, social justice, education, or the arts, this unique ability has the power to shape the world in profound and lasting ways. The following sections will explore the core strengths, natural aptitudes, and practical applications of Visionary Genius, providing insights into how this remarkable talent can be cultivated and applied in various fields.

Core Strengths of Visionary Geniuses

Visionary Geniuses thrive through key strengths such as big-picture thinking, innovation, strategic problem-solving, and future-oriented perspectives. They excel at understanding the broader context, seeking innovative solutions, and anticipating long-term outcomes. Their strategic approach ensures that their ideas are both revolutionary and sustainable.

Big-picture thinking allows Visionary Geniuses to see beyond immediate circumstances and understand how different elements interconnect. For example, Steve Jobs envisioned a world where technology seamlessly integrated into everyday life, leading to products like the iPhone that revolutionized communication (Isaacson 2011). Similarly, Wangari Maathai recognized that environmental sustainability was essential for social and economic well-being, prompting her to found the Green Belt Movement (Maathai 2006).

Innovation is another hallmark of Visionary Geniuses. They challenge the status quo and seek creative solutions to complex problems. Ada Lovelace, for instance, saw the potential of Charles Babbage's mechanical computer beyond simple calculations, envisioning its use for more complex tasks and laying the foundation for modern computing (Stein 1985). Similarly, entrepreneurs like Oprah Winfrey have transformed their industries by introducing new ways of connecting with and empowering people (Kelley 2010).

Strategic problem-solving involves analyzing trends and anticipating challenges before they arise. Jeff Bezos illustrated this strength by recognizing the potential of e-commerce long before it became mainstream (Stone 2013). He created a platform that reshaped global commerce by strategically expanding Amazon's offerings and streamlining logistics. Malala Yousafzai's strategic advocacy for girls' education illustrates how visionary thinking can drive social change as she influences policy and public opinion worldwide (Yousafzai & Lamb 2013).

A future-oriented mindset enables Visionary Geniuses to anticipate emerging opportunities and potential threats. They constantly scan the horizon for new developments and adjust their strategies accordingly. For example, a visionary tech leader's focus on sustainable energy and space exploration reflects a belief that these areas are critical to humanity's future (Vance 2015). Similarly, Maya Angelou's work as a poet and activist anticipated societal shifts toward greater equality and understanding (Angelou 1969).

The core strengths of Visionary Geniuses allow them to see beyond the present, imagine new possibilities, and develop solutions that have a lasting impact. By combining big-picture thinking, innovation, strategic problem-solving, and a future-oriented mindset, these individuals continue to shape the world in transformative ways.

Core Strength	Description
Big-Picture Thinking	Ability to see the overarching context and long-term implications.
Innovation	Challenging the status quo and seeking creative solutions.
Strategic Problem-Solving	Analyzing trends to address current and future challenges.
Future-Oriented Mindset	Constantly anticipating emerging opportunities and potential threats.

Natural Aptitudes of Visionary Geniuses

Natural aptitudes such as curiosity, creativity, analytical thinking, empathy, and resilience fuel the success of Visionary Geniuses. Their relentless desire to learn and explore drives innovation, while their ability to break down complex problems enables effective solutions. Empathy allows them to create impactful, people-centered innovations, and resilience ensures they persist through adversity.

Curiosity is a hallmark of visionary individuals. For example, George Washington Carver's insatiable curiosity about agriculture led to ground-breaking innovations that transformed farming practices in the United States, especially for African American farmers. His research into crop rotation and alternative products from peanuts and sweet potatoes advanced science and uplifted marginalized communities (Kremer 2011).

Creativity involves thinking outside the box and generating innovative solutions. In Latino culture, artists like Frida Kahlo channeled their creativity into works that challenged societal norms and provided a voice for historically excluded populations (Herrera 2002). In the realm of music, innovators like Celia Cruz redefined salsa, blending traditional rhythms with modern elements to create a genre that resonated worldwide.

Analytical thinking allows Visionary Geniuses to break down complex problems into manageable components. Civil rights leaders like Dr. Martin Luther King Jr. used this aptitude to strategically dismantle racism (Branch 1988). His ability to analyze societal structures and devise nonviolent protest methods helped catalyze significant social change. Similarly, Sonia Sotomayor's analytical skills enabled her to navigate the complexities of the legal system, ultimately becoming the first Latina Supreme Court Justice in the United States (Sotomayor 2013).

Empathy is essential for creating solutions that address the needs of others. Oprah Winfrey's empathy and ability to connect with diverse audiences made her a transformative figure in media, fostering conversations on race, gender, and personal growth (Kelley 2010). Cesar Chavez, driven by empathy for farm workers' struggles, co-founded the United Farm Workers union, advocating for better wages and working conditions (Griswold del Castillo & Garcia 1995).

Resilience is the determination to overcome obstacles and persist despite adversity. Maya Angelou's resilience, reflected in her poetry and memoirs, inspired countless individuals to confront personal and societal challenges (Angelou 1969). In sports, Roberto Clemente overcame racial barriers in Major League Baseball, becoming a trailblazer for Latino athletes and dedicating his life to humanitarian causes (Marán 2010).

These natural aptitudes, curiosity, creativity, analytical thinking, empathy, and resilience, empower Visionary Geniuses to envision a better future and take the steps needed to make it a reality. By exploring relatable stories, we better understand how these qualities shape individuals who drive lasting change.

Aptitude	Description
Curiosity	The constant drive to explore new ideas and knowledge.
Creativity	Thinking outside the box to generate innovative solutions.
Analytical Thinking	Breaking down complex problems into manageable components.
Empathy	Understanding and addressing the needs of others.
Resilience	Overcoming obstacles and maintaining determination.

Common Professions and Applications

Visionary Geniuses often excel in professions requiring innovation and long-term planning, such as entrepreneurship, leadership, futurism, invention, policy-making, and venture capitalism. Their ability to connect ideas and foresee future developments enables them to disrupt industries and shape societal progress.

Visionary Geniuses drive transformative change in education by developing new teaching methods and creating more inclusive learning environments. For example, Maria Montessori revolutionized early childhood education with her innovative approach, emphasizing independence and hands-on learning (Montessori 1964). Her methods have become a global standard, proving that reimagining education can have a lasting impact.

Visionary Geniuses often emerge as entrepreneurs and CEOs who build innovative businesses that challenge traditional industries. Daymond John, founder of FUBU, exemplifies this by transforming the fashion industry and empowering minority entrepreneurs (John & Paisner 2007). His success story illustrates how combining creativity with strategic thinking can disrupt markets and inspire future generations.

Futurists play a critical role in analyzing and predicting trends to guide decision-making. Alvin Toffler, author of *Future Shock,* helped society understand the rapid changes brought by technology, influencing both public policy and business strategy (Toffler 1970). Similarly, inventors like Madam C.J. Walker, the first African American woman to become a self-made millionaire, developed beauty products that met a market need while empowering women of color (Bundles 2001).

Politicians who possess Visionary Genius craft policies to address long-term societal challenges. Barack Obama's leadership as the first African American President of the United States exemplified how forward-thinking policies can promote social equity and global cooperation (Obama 2006). His emphasis on healthcare reform, environmental sustainability, and education reshaped national priorities.

Business strategists design long-term strategies that ensure sustainable growth. For example, Ursula Burns, former CEO of Xerox, led the company through a digital transformation that positioned it for success in the modern era (Burns 2021). Her strategic vision revitalized Xerox and paved the way for greater diversity in corporate leadership.

Thought leaders shape public discourse and influence societal values. In the entertainment industry, Ava DuVernay's films, such as *Selma* and *13th*, have sparked conversations about race, justice, and equality, demonstrating the power of storytelling to drive social change (DuVernay 2014). Similarly, Lin-Manuel Miranda redefined theater with *Hamilton*, blending history, hip-hop, and diverse casting to create a cultural phenomenon (Isherwood 2015).

Research scientists expand human knowledge through pioneering discoveries. George Washington Carver's agricultural innovations improved farming practices and economic conditions for countless communities (Kremer 2011). His ability to see the potential in everyday resources exemplifies how visionary thinking can create practical solutions with lasting benefits.

Change agents lead social movements that drive positive change. Cesar Chavez's advocacy for farmworkers' rights not only improved labor conditions but also inspired future generations to fight for social justice (Griswold del

Castillo & Garcia 1995). Similarly, Malala Yousafzai's global campaign for girls' education has challenged cultural barriers and empowered young women worldwide (Yousafzai & Lamb 2013).

Venture capitalists invest in startups poised to reshape entire industries. For example, Arlan Hamilton, founder of Backstage Capital, has disrupted the venture capital industry by championing underrepresented entrepreneurs, proving that investing in diverse talent can drive innovation and economic growth (Hamilton 2020).

Visionary Geniuses thrive in professions that allow them to leverage their creativity, strategic thinking, and future-oriented mindset. Whether in educa-tion, business, or entertainment, their ability to connect ideas and anticipate trends enables them to shape industries, inspire societal progress, and create a more inclusive and innovative world.

Profession	Application
Entrepreneurs	Building innovative businesses that challenge traditional industries.
CEOs	Leading organizations with future-focused strategies.
Futurists	Analyzing and predicting trends to guide decision-making.
Inventors	Developing technologies that revolutionize everyday life.
Politicians	Crafting policies to address long-term societal challenges.
Business Strategists	Designing strategies that ensure sustainable growth.
Thought Leaders	Shaping public discourse and influencing societal values.
Research Scientists	Expanding human knowledge through pioneering discoveries.

| Change Agents | Leading social movements that drive positive change. |
| Venture Capitalists | Investing in startups poised to reshape entire industries. |

Developing Your Visionary Genius

Developing Visionary Genius involves expanding knowledge, thinking long-term, and embracing creativity. Individuals can cultivate this mindset by continuously learning, connecting disparate ideas, and analyzing trends to anticipate future developments. Building resilience and inspiring others are essential components of this journey.

Expand your knowledge by immersing yourself in diverse fields of study. Read books, attend seminars, and engage with thought leaders across various industries. For example, a business leader might study philosophy to gain new perspectives on ethics and decision-making. This cross-disciplinary approach fosters innovative thinking and opens up new possibilities.

Thinking long-term requires shifting focus from immediate rewards to lasting impact. Set goals that contribute to long-term success, for yourself and society. Entrepreneurs like Daymond John and visionaries like Oprah Winfrey achieved success by remaining dedicated to their long-term visions, even when faced with short-term obstacles. Keeping your eyes on the bigger picture ensures that your efforts lead to meaningful and enduring results.

Connecting the dots is about identifying relationships between seemingly unrelated concepts. Pay attention to patterns and trends, and consider how different ideas might intersect. Steve Jobs famously connected technology with design, revolutionizing how people interact with devices. Similarly, artists like Lin-Manuel Miranda combined history and hip-hop to create groundbreaking works that resonate across generations.

Embracing creativity means challenging conventional thinking and exploring new solutions. Cultivate a mindset that welcomes experimentation and is unafraid of failure. Innovation often comes from taking risks and thinking outside the box. For example, George Washington Carver's creative approach to agriculture led to breakthroughs that benefited farmers and the environment.

Developing strategic thinking involves analyzing current trends to anticipate future developments. Stay informed about changes in your field and consider how they might impact the future. Visionary leaders like Ursula Burns transformed their industries by recognizing opportunities and developing forward-thinking strategies. Practice strategic thinking by regularly assessing both short-term challenges and long-term opportunities.

Building resilience is essential for overcoming setbacks and persisting despite challenges. Understand that failure is a natural part of the learning process and use it as an opportunity to grow. Despite facing life-threatening opposition, Malala Yousafzai's unwavering commitment to girls' education exemplifies the power of resilience in achieving long-term goals.

Finally, inspiring others is key to turning your vision into reality. Share your ideas passionately and clearly, motivating others to join you on your journey. Effective communication and empathy are essential for building support and fostering collaboration. Leaders like Barack Obama and Ava DuVernay have used their platforms to inspire positive change and empower others to pursue their visions.

By following these practical steps, expanding knowledge, thinking long-term, connecting the dots, embracing creativity, developing strategic thinking, building resilience, and inspiring others, you can cultivate your Visionary Genius and impact the world.

Development Strategy	Description
Expand Knowledge	Continuously explore diverse fields of study.
Think Long-Term	Focus on long-term impact rather than short-term gains.
Connect the Dots	Identify connections between seemingly unrelated ideas.
Embrace Creativity	Challenge conventional thinking to discover new solutions.
Develop Strategic Thinking	Analyze current trends to anticipate future developments.
Build Resilience	Learn from setbacks and persist despite challenges.
Inspire Others	Communicate your vision to motivate and guide others.

Shaping the Future

Visionary Geniuses are essential in shaping the future, using their foresight and creativity to drive progress. By honing their strengths, embracing diverse perspectives, and developing strategic solutions, individuals can contribute to an innovative, sustainable, and inclusive future. As the world evolves, the ability to think beyond the present and pioneer new possibilities will remain vital in creating a better tomorrow.

Chapter References

Angelou, Maya. *I Know Why the Caged Bird Sings.* Random House, 1969.

Branch, Taylor. P*arting the Waters: America in the King Years 1954–63.* Simon & Schuster, 1988.

Bundles, *A'Lelia. On Her Own Ground: The Life and Times of Madam C. J. Walker.* Scribner, 2001.

Burns, Ursula. *Where You Are Is Not Who You Are: A Memoir.* Amistad, 2021.

DuVernay, Ava, director. *Selma.* Paramount Pictures, 2014.

Griswold del Castillo, Richard, and Richard Garcia. *Cesar Chavez: A Triumph of Spirit.* University of Oklahoma Press, 1995.

Hamilton, Arlan. *It's About Damn Time: How to Turn Being Underestimated into Your Greatest Advantage.* Currency, 2020.

Herrera, Hayden. *Frida: A Biography of Frida Kahlo.* Harper Perennial, 2002.

Isaacson, Walter. *Steve Jobs.* Simon & Schuster, 2011.

Isherwood, Charles. "Review: 'Hamilton,' Young Rebels Changing History and Theater." *The New York Times*, August 6, 2015.

John, Daymond, and Daniel Paisner. *Display of Power: How FUBU Changed a World of Fashion, Branding and Lifestyle.* Naked Ink, 2007.

Kelley, Kitty. *Oprah: A Biography.* Crown Archetype, 2010.

Kremer, Gary R. *George Washington Carver: In His Own Words.* 2nd ed. University of Missouri Press, 2011.

Maathai, Wangari. *Unbowed: A Memoir.* Knopf, 2006.

Marán, Roberto. *Clemente: The Passion and Grace of Baseball's Last Hero.* Touchstone, 2010.

Montessori, Maria. *The Montessori Method.* Schocken Books, 1964.

Obama, Barack. *The Audacity of Hope: Thoughts on Reclaiming the American Dream.* Crown, 2006.

Sotomayor, Sonia. *My Beloved World.* Vintage, 2013.

Stein, Dorothy. *Ada: A Life and Legacy.* MIT Press, 1985.

Stone, Brad. *The Everything Store: Jeff Bezos and the Age of Amazon.* Little, Brown and Company, 2013.

Toffler, Alvin. *Future Shock.* Random House, 1970.

Vance, Ashlee. *Elon Musk: Tesla, SpaceX, and the Quest for a Fantastic Future.* HarperCollins, 2015.

Yousafzai, Malala, and Christina Lamb. *I Am Malala: The Girl Who Stood Up for Education and Was Shot by the Taliban.* Little, Brown and Company, 2013.

Chapter 3

The Power of
RELATIONAL GENIUS

Defining Relational Genius

Relational Geniuses possess a remarkable ability to understand, connect with, and inspire others. Their emotional intelligence, empathy, and leadership skills enable them to navigate complex social dynamics and build meaningful relationships (Goleman 1995). This form of genius is essential in professions that involve guiding and supporting others, such as teaching, counseling, coaching, and community organizing.

At its core, Relational Genius is about recognizing and responding to the emotions and needs of others. For example, a teacher who notices a student struggling academically and emotionally demonstrates this ability by providing both educational support and compassionate guidance. Similarly, a coach who motivates their team through strategy while fostering trust and camaraderie exemplifies Relational Genius.

This type of intelligence is evident in everyday life as well. Consider a parent who senses when their child needs reassurance or encouragement or a friend who offers a listening ear and words of comfort during difficult times.

These moments of connection, though often subtle, have a profound impact on relationships and well-being. For instance, a community organizer who brings diverse groups together to address local issues must understand different perspectives, build consensus, and inspire collective action, all hallmarks of Relational Genius (Huerta 2008).

Relational Geniuses also excel at building and maintaining trust. A manager who creates a supportive work environment where employees feel valued and heard fosters both morale and productivity. In customer service, an agent who listens attentively and empathizes with a customer's concerns can turn a negative experience into a positive one, strengthening brand loyalty. These examples highlight how Relational Genius extends beyond personal interactions to shape professional success and community cohesion.

Moreover, Relational Genius is closely linked to emotional intelligence, the ability to recognize, understand, and manage one's own emotions while empathizing with others (Goleman 1995). This combination of self-awareness and social awareness allows individuals to navigate complex interpersonal situations gracefully and effectively. For example, a social worker who remains calm and compassionate in the face of a client's distress exhibits both emotional resilience and empathetic connection, empowering the client to overcome challenges.

Relational Genius is the ability to create meaningful connections, foster mutual understanding, and inspire others to reach their potential. It is a skill that can be cultivated and refined, enriching both personal and professional relationships. By mastering the art of empathy, communication, and leadership, individuals can build stronger communities, enhance collaboration, and make a lasting impact on the world around them.

Core Strengths of Relational Geniuses

Relational Geniuses excel in several key areas that enable them to foster connection and promote personal growth. These strengths are illustrated through the lives and work of famous figures who have spotlighted exceptional relational abilities.

Emotional intelligence is exemplified by Barack Obama, whose ability to remain composed and empathetic under pressure helped him connect with diverse audiences (Obama 2006). His speeches often resonated on a personal level, fostering a sense of unity and hope. Similarly, Oprah Winfrey's emotional intelligence allows her to connect deeply with her audience, creating a space where people feel understood and valued (Kelley 2010).

Empathy is at the heart of Relational Genius, as reflected by Mother Teresa, who dedicated her life to serving the poor and underprivileged (Scaria 2016). Her profound empathy enabled her to provide not only physical aid but also emotional and spiritual comfort. In the realm of literature, Maya Angelou's poetry and prose captured the human experience with compassion and insight, touching the hearts of readers worldwide (Angelou 1969).

Connection involves building authentic relationships and creating environ-ments where people feel valued. Fred Rogers, known for his television show *Mister Rogers' Neighborhood,* embodied this strength by teaching children to understand and manage their emotions (King 2018). His gentle, compassionate approach made every viewer feel seen and accepted. Nelson Mandela also exemplified this strength by fostering reconciliation and unity in post-apartheid South Africa, building bridges between commu-nities that had long been divided (Mandela 1995).

Leadership is essential for guiding and inspiring others. Martin Luther King Jr. led the civil rights movement with a vision of justice and equality, inspiring millions to join the struggle for human rights (Branch 1988). His ability to communicate a powerful, compassionate message helped unite people from all walks of life. Similarly, Malala Yousafzai's leadership in advocating for girls' education has inspired a global movement, demonstrating that even young voices can drive significant change (Yousafzai & Lamb 2013).

Community building creates a sense of belonging and shared purpose within groups and organizations. Through his work with farmworkers, Cesar Chavez built a community based on solidarity and mutual support (Griswold del Castillo & Garcia 1995). His leadership improved working conditions and empowered individuals to advocate for their rights. In sports, LeBron James has used his platform to promote social justice and community development, creating programs that support underserved youth and advocate for equality (Brennan 2020).

These examples illustrate how the core strengths of Relational Genius, emotional intelligence, empathy, connection, leadership, and community building, can be applied to inspire positive change and foster meaningful relationships. By studying these figures, individuals can learn to develop their relational abilities and make a lasting impact in their personal and professional lives.

Core Strength	Description
Emotional Intelligence	Understanding and managing one's emotions while recognizing and responding to the feelings of others.
Empathy	The ability to understand and share the feelings of others and foster compassion and trust.
Connection	Building authentic relationships and creating environments where people feel valued and understood.
Leadership	Guiding and inspiring others to achieve their goals and realize their potential.
Community Building	Creating a sense of belonging and shared purpose within groups and organizations.

Natural Aptitudes of Relational Geniuses

Relational Geniuses possess inherent qualities that enable them to thrive in interpersonal settings. These natural aptitudes, active listening, communication, compassion, adaptability, and conflict resolution, are each illustrated through practical examples from education, business, and entertainment.

Active listening is essential for building trust and understanding. In education, teachers like Jaime Escalante, known for his work with underprivileged students, listened to his students' struggles and provided the support they needed to succeed (Stand and Deliver 1988). In business, leaders like Howard Schultz of Starbucks have emphasized listening to employees and customers to create a culture of respect and collaboration (Schultz & Gordon 2011). In entertainment, talk show hosts like Oprah Winfrey use active listening to create a space where guests feel valued and heard (Kelley 2010).

Communication involves expressing ideas clearly and empathetically. Educators like Rita Pierson, who famously said, "Every child deserves a champion," demonstrate how compassionate communication can inspire students to believe in themselves (Pierson 2013). In the business world, leaders like Sheryl Sandberg, COO of Meta, use clear and empathetic communication to foster open dialogue and build inclusive workplaces (Sandberg 2013). In entertainment, actors like Denzel Washington use their platforms to communicate messages of resilience, hope, and social justice, connecting with audiences worldwide (Harris 2021).

Compassion is about showing genuine care for others. Teachers like Anne Sullivan, who taught Helen Keller to communicate despite her disabilities, exemplify how compassion can unlock human potential (Lash 1980). In business, philanthropists like Melinda French Gates use their resources to improve global health and education (Gates 2022). In entertainment, figures like Robin Williams used their talent to bring joy and laughter, demonstrating the profound impact of compassion in everyday life (Itzkoff 2018).

Adaptability is crucial for meeting the needs of diverse individuals and situations. In education, teachers constantly adjust their methods to meet the needs of different learners. In business, entrepreneurs like Daymond John of FUBU adapted to changing market trends, building a brand that resonated with a global audience (John & Paisner 2007). In entertainment, artists like Beyoncé continually evolve their music and performances, connecting with audiences across generations and cultures (Gabler 2019).

Conflict resolution is vital for maintaining harmony and fostering under-standing. Educators often mediate conflicts between students, teaching them to resolve disagreements constructively. In business, leaders like Satya Nadella, CEO of Microsoft, have transformed corporate culture by promoting empathy and collaboration (Meisler 2021). In entertainment, filmmakers like Ava DuVernay use their work to address social injustices, encouraging dialogue and empathy (DuVernay 2016).

These practical examples show how the natural aptitudes of Relational Genius, active listening, communication, compassion, adaptability, and conflict resolution, are essential in education, business, and entertainment. By cultivating these qualities, individuals can build stronger relationships, foster understanding, and inspire positive changes in their personal and professional lives.

Aptitude	Description
Active Listening	Fully engaging with others, demonstrating attentiveness and understanding.
Communication	Expressing ideas clearly and empathetically and fostering open dialogue.
Compassion	Showing genuine care and concern for the well-being of others.
Adaptability	Adjusting one's approach to meet the needs of different individuals and situations.
Conflict Resolution	Mediating disputes and promoting harmony through understanding and compromise.

Common Professions and Applications

Relational Geniuses are found in professions that require strong interpersonal skills and a broader understanding of human behavior. Their ability to connect with others and provide guidance makes them invaluable in various fields. For example, therapists like Carl Rogers revolutionized psychotherapy by emphasizing empathy and unconditional positive regard, helping individuals navigate emotional and psychological challenges (Rogers 1961). Counselors, such as school counselors, provide guidance and support to students and families, promoting mental well-being and academic success.

Teachers like Jaime Escalante inspire and educate students, fostering both academic and personal growth. Social workers, such as Jane Addams, advocate for individuals and communities to improve their well-being through compassionate support and advocacy (Knight 2005). Religious leaders like Desmond Tutu offer spiritual guidance and create supportive faith communities that promote compassion and justice (Tutu 2011).

Coaches, including life coaches and athletic coaches, empower individuals to reach their personal and professional goals through motivation and guidance. Human resources professionals build positive workplace cultures by supporting employee development and fostering collaboration. Diplomats like Kofi Annan facilitate communication and cooperation between nations, promoting global peace and understanding (Annan 2012).

Customer relations managers play a key role in ensuring positive interactions between businesses and their customers, enhancing customer satisfaction and loyalty. Community organizers, such as Dolores Huerta, lead social movements that advocate for social justice and foster collective action (Huerta 2008). Conflict mediators use their skills to resolve disputes and promote harmony through understanding and compromise, helping individuals and groups navigate difficult situations.

These examples illustrate the diverse applications of Relational Genius across multiple work disciplines. By leveraging their emotional intelligence, empathy, and communication skills, individuals in these professions can build meaningful relationships, foster collaboration, and inspire positive change in their communities and organizations.

Profession	Application
Therapists	Help individuals navigate emotional and psychological challenges.
Counselors	Provide support and guidance to individuals and families.
Teachers	Inspire and educate students, fostering both academic and personal growth.
Social Workers	Advocate for individuals and communities to improve their well-being.
Religious Leaders	Offer spiritual guidance and create supportive faith communities.
Coaches	Empower individuals to reach their personal and professional goals.
Human Resources Professionals	Build positive workplace cultures and support employee development.
Diplomats	Facilitate communication and cooperation between nations.
Customer Relations Managers	Ensure positive interactions between businesses and their customers.

Community Organizers	Lead social movements and foster collective action.
Conflict Mediators	Resolve disputes and promote understanding and collaboration.

Developing Your Relational Genius

Developing Relational Genius involves straightforward, practical steps that anyone can apply in their daily life. By practicing these strategies consistently, individuals can enhance their ability to connect with others, foster trust, and inspire positive change.

One key step is practicing active listening, which means focusing intently on the speaker, maintaining eye contact, and responding thoughtfully. For example, a teacher who listens carefully to a student's concerns can provide better guidance and support. In the workplace, a manager who actively listens to their team members fosters an environment where employees feel heard and valued.

Enhancing emotional intelligence involves becoming more aware of one's own emotions and learning to recognize and respond to the feelings of others. For instance, a counselor who understands their client's emotional state can offer more effective support. Similarly, a coach who senses an athlete is anxious can provide the encouragement needed to boost their confidence.

Building authentic connections requires fostering relationships based on trust, empathy, and mutual respect. A community organizer who builds genuine relationships with local residents can inspire collective action. Likewise, a business leader who connects personally with their employees creates a more cohesive and motivated team.

Improving communication skills involves expressing thoughts clearly and empathetically. For example, a diplomat who communicates with clarity and empathy can build stronger international relationships. Transparent and compassionate communication in customer service helps resolve issues and strengthens customer loyalty.

Cultivating compassion means approaching others with kindness and a genuine desire to help. A social worker who shows compassion toward their clients can help them feel understood and supported. In everyday life, simple acts of kindness, such as offering a listening ear or lending a helping hand, can strengthen relationships and build trust.

Developing conflict resolution skills is essential for maintaining harmony and promoting understanding. A conflict mediator who helps individuals find common ground can resolve disputes and restore relationships. Similarly, a teacher who teaches students to resolve disagreements constructively fosters a more positive classroom environment.

Leading with empathy involves understanding and addressing the needs and motivations of others. A coach who motivates their team by recognizing each player's unique strengths can inspire better performance. A religious leader who empathizes with their congregation's challenges can provide more meaningful guidance and support.

By applying these practical steps, active listening, enhancing emotional intelligence, building authentic connections, improving communication skills, cultivating compassion, developing conflict resolution skills, and leading with empathy, anyone can develop their Relational Genius. These qualities help individuals make a lasting impact on their personal and professional relationships.

Development Strategy	Description
Practice Active Listening	Focus on truly hearing and understanding what others are saying.
Enhance Emotional Intelligence	Develop awareness of your own emotions and learn to recognize and respond to the moods of others.
Build Authentic Connections	Foster genuine relationships based on trust, empathy, and mutual respect.
Improve Communication Skills	Learn to express your thoughts clearly and empathetically.
Cultivate Compassion	Approach others with kindness and a genuine desire to help.
Develop Conflict Resolution Skills	Learn techniques for resolving disputes and promoting understanding.
Lead with Empathy	Inspire and guide others by understanding their needs and motivations.

Strengthening Human Connection

Relational Geniuses are vital in building a more compassionate and connected world. Their emotional intelligence, empathy, and leadership skills enable them to guide others, foster community, and inspire positive change. By developing these abilities, individuals can enhance their relationships, support those around them, and contribute to a more understanding and inclusive society. As we navigate an increasingly complex world, the power of human connection remains essential to our collective well-being and progress.

Chapter References

Annan, Kofi. *Interventions: A Life in War and Peace.* Penguin, 2012.

Angelou, Maya. *I Know Why the Caged Bird Sings.* Random House, 1969.

Branch, Taylor. *Parting the Waters: America in the King Years 1954–63.* Simon & Schuster, 1988.

Brennan, Christine. "LeBron James Continues to Show Leadership Off the Court." *USA Today,* June 4, 2020. https://www.usatoday.com

DuVernay, Ava, director. *13th.* Netflix, 2016.

Gabler, Neal. *Beyoncé: The Making of a Pop Icon.* HarperCollins, 2019.

Gates, Melinda French. *The Moment of Lift: How Empowering Women Changes the World.* Flatiron Books, 2022.

Goleman, Daniel. *Emotional Intelligence: Why It Can Matter More Than IQ. Bantam Books*, 1995.

Griswold del Castillo, Richard, and Richard Garcia. *Cesar Chavez: A Triumph of Spirit.* University of Oklahoma Press, 1995.

Harris, Aaron. *Denzel Washington: A Biography.* Greenwood, 2021.

Huerta, Dolores. *Dolores Huerta: A Hero to Migrant Workers.* HarperCollins, 2008.

Itzkoff, Dave. *Robin.* Henry Holt and Co., 2018.

John, Daymond, and Daniel Paisner. *Display of Power: How FUBU Changed a World of Fashion, Branding and Lifestyle.* Naked Ink, 2007.

Kelley, Kitty. *Oprah: A Biography.* Crown Archetype, 2010.

King, Maxwell L. *The Good Neighbor: The Life and Work of Fred Rogers.* Abrams Press, 2018.

Knight, Louise W. *Citizen: Jane Addams and the Struggle for Democracy.* University of Chicago Press, 2005.

Lash, Joseph P. *Helen and Teacher: The Story of Helen Keller and Anne Sullivan Macy.* Delacorte Press, 1980.

Mandela, Nelson. *Long Walk to Freedom: The Autobiography of Nelson Mandela.* Little, Brown and Company, 1995.

Meisler, Adam. *Satya Nadella: The Reimagining of Microsoft.* Harper Business, 2021.

Obama, Barack. *The Audacity of Hope: Thoughts on Reclaiming the American Dream.* Crown, 2006.

Pierson, Rita. "Every Child Needs a Champion." *TED Talk, 2013.*
https://www.ted.com

Rogers, Carl R. *On Becoming a Person: A Therapist's View of Psychotherapy.* Houghton Mifflin, 1961.

Sandberg, Sheryl. *Lean In: Women, Work, and the Will to Lead.* Knopf, 2013.
Stand and Deliver. Warner Bros., 1988.

Tutu, Desmond. *God Is Not a Christian: And Other Provocations.* HarperOne, 2011.

Yousafzai, Malala, and Christina Lamb. *I Am Malala: The Girl Who Stood Up for Education and Was Shot by the Taliban.* Little, Brown and Company, 2013

Chapter 4

The Power of EXECUTION GENIUS

Defining Execution Genius

Execution Geniuses possess an exceptional ability to organize, plan, and execute complex projects with precision and efficiency. Their talent lies in structuring processes for maximum productivity, analyzing data to make informed decisions, and managing logistics to ensure seamless operations (Drucker 1999). This form of genius is vital in fields that require meticulous planning and operational excellence, such as project management, engineering, business analysis, and supply chain management.

In everyday life, Execution Genius is evident in individuals who can break down large tasks into manageable steps, ensuring that projects are completed on time and within budget. For example, a teacher planning a semester-long curriculum must organize lessons, assignments, and classroom activities to maximize student learning. Similarly, an event coordinator managing a large-scale conference must oversee scheduling, logistics, and vendor relationships to ensure a seamless experience for attendees.

Execution Geniuses excel at identifying the most efficient way to achieve their goals. A business analyst might use data to pinpoint inefficiencies in a company's workflow, developing solutions that improve productivity and reduce costs. Meanwhile, a supply chain manager ensures that goods are delivered to customers quickly and cost-effectively, optimizing transportation routes and inventory levels.

Data-driven decision-making is a hallmark of Execution Genius. For example, a financial analyst uses performance metrics to assess investment opportunities, balancing risk and reward to maximize returns. In sports, coaches analyze player statistics to develop winning strategies, adjusting their game plans based on real-time data.

In the entertainment industry, Execution Genius is essential for delivering high-quality productions on schedule and within budget. A film director like Christopher Nolan must coordinate actors, crew members, and special effects teams, ensuring that each element of the production aligns with the overall vision (Robinson 2014). Similarly, a music producer oversees the recording process, guiding artists and sound engineers to create a polished final product (Passman 2015).

Whether managing a corporate project, leading a construction team, or organizing a community event, Execution Geniuses bring structure, clarity, and efficiency to every task. Their ability to plan, execute, and optimize processes ensures that goals are achieved and challenges are overcome.

Core Strengths of Execution Geniuses

Execution Geniuses excel in several key areas that enable them to drive efficiency and achieve results. Their strengths are often demonstrated through real-world examples of entrepreneurs who took small ideas and grew them into successful ventures.

Organization is essential for maintaining order and productivity. For example, Sara Blakely, the founder of Spanx, started with a simple idea for shapewear and meticulously organized her business operations to scale her company globally (Blakely 2012). Efficiency is about using resources effectively. Howard Schultz transformed Starbucks from a small coffee shop into a global brand by streamlining operations and enhancing the customer experience (Schultz & Yang 2011).

Planning involves developing step-by-step strategies to achieve long-term goals. Steve Jobs exemplified this strength by creating a product roadmap that guided Apple from a niche computer maker to a global technology leader (Isaacson 2011). Execution is about turning plans into action. Oprah Winfrey built her media empire by consistently delivering high-quality content, demonstrating exceptional follow-through and dedication (Kelley 2010).

Data-driven decision-making allows Execution Geniuses to evaluate performance and make informed improvements. Jeff Bezos built Amazon into an e-commerce giant using data analytics to optimize supply chains and personalize customer experiences (Stone 2013).

These examples illustrate how entrepreneurs use core strengths, such as organization, efficiency, planning, execution, and data-driven decision-making, to grow small ideas into thriving businesses. Their success highlights the importance of operational excellence and strategic thinking in achieving long-term goals.

Core Strength	Description
Organization	Structuring tasks and processes to maximize efficiency and productivity.
Efficiency	Using resources effectively to achieve goals with minimal waste.
Planning	Developing comprehensive strategies to achieve long-term objectives.
Execution	Implementing plans and ensuring that tasks are completed successfully.
Data-Driven Decision-Making	Using data and analytics to guide decisions and improve outcomes.

Natural Aptitudes of Execution Geniuses

Execution Geniuses possess inherent qualities that enable them to excel in operational roles. Their abilities are often exemplified through the successes of young entrepreneurs who leverage technology to create thriving businesses, social advocates who use innovative methods to drive societal change, and individuals who revolutionize industries by rethinking established practices.

Attention to detail is essential for ensuring accuracy and precision. For example, Mark Zuckerberg's focus on user experience and platform functionality helped transform Facebook from a college networking site into a global social media powerhouse (Kirkpatrick 2010). **Logical thinking** allows Execution Geniuses to analyze problems and develop practical solutions. Young entrepreneur Melanie Perkins co-founded Canva, a graphic design platform that simplifies design processes for non professionals, making high-quality design accessible to everyone (Perkins 2021).

Time management is critical for meeting deadlines without compromising quality. Jack Ma, the founder of Alibaba, balanced rapid growth with efficient operations, scaling the company into one of the world's largest e-commerce platforms (Clark 2016). **Adaptability** enables Execution Geniuses to adjust strategies in response to challenges. Malala Yousafzai adapted her advocacy methods to reach global audiences, using social media and public speaking to advance girls' education (Yousafzai & Lamb 2013). **Accountability** involves taking responsibility for outcomes and ensuring that goals are met.

These examples illustrate how Execution Geniuses apply their natural aptitudes to achieve success in various fields, from technology and business to social advocacy and industry transformation.

Aptitude	Description
Attention to Detail	Ensuring that every component of a project is accurate and precise.
Logical Thinking	Analyzing problems and developing practical solutions.
Time Management	Prioritizing tasks to meet deadlines without compromising quality.
Adaptability	Adjusting plans and strategies to address unexpected challenges.
Accountability	Taking responsibility for outcomes and ensuring that goals are met.

Common Professions and Applications

Execution Geniuses thrive in roles that require strong organizational and analytical skills. Their ability to optimize processes and manage logistics is essential across various industries, as highlighted by lesser-known public figures who have made a significant impact.

Project managers like Dorothy Vaughan, a NASA mathematician featured in the book and movie *Hidden Figures*, ensured that critical space missions succeeded by managing complex calculations and overseeing teams (Shetterly 2016). Engineers like Lewis Howard Latimer, who improved electric light technology, used their expertise to design systems that changed everyday life (Haber 1991). Business analysts like Maggie Lena Walker, the first African American woman to charter a bank, analyzed financial data to guide business decisions and support her community (Morris 2003).

Supply chain managers like Charles Richard Drew revolutionized blood storage and distribution, saving countless lives during World War II (Rogers 2013). Financial analysts like Madam C.J. Walker, who built a beauty empire, used strategic investments to grow her business and support social causes (Bundles 2001). Military leaders like General Benjamin O. Davis Jr. led the Tuskegee Airmen, demonstrating excellence in coordination and strategy (Davis 1991).

Accountants such as Mary T. Washington Wylie, the first African American woman CPA, ensured financial accuracy and compliance while breaking barriers in the accounting profession (Lemke 1994). Quality control experts like Frederick McKinley Jones, who developed refrigeration systems, ensured that perishable goods could be transported safely (U.S. Department of Energy 2016). Process improvement specialists like Grace Hopper, a pioneer in computer programming, optimized workflows that laid the foundation for modern computing (Beyer 2009). Logisticians like Harriet Tubman, who managed the Underground Railroad, used strategic planning and precise execution to guide people to freedom (Clinton 2004).

These examples highlight how Execution Geniuses across various professions have used their skills to drive innovation, improve efficiency, and create lasting change.

Profession	Application
Project Managers	Overseeing projects from initiation to completion, ensuring efficiency.
Engineers	Designing and implementing systems and structures.
Business Analysts	Analyzing data to improve business processes and decision-making.
Supply Chain Managers	Managing the flow of goods and services to ensure timely delivery.
Financial Analysts	Using data to guide investment and financial decisions.
Military Leaders	Coordinating complex operations and ensuring mission success.
Accountants	Maintaining financial accuracy and compliance.
Quality Control Experts	Ensuring that products meet industry standards and customer expectations.
Process Improvement Specialists	Identifying inefficiencies and optimizing workflows.
Logisticians	Managing transportation and distribution to ensure timely delivery.

Developing Your Execution Genius

Developing Execution Genius involves cultivating specific skills and adopting practical strategies. The following steps provide a detailed, straight-forward approach to building these capabilities, supported by examples from various fields.

Master organization by using tools and systems to keep tasks structured and information accessible. For example, project management software like Trello or Asana helps teams track progress, assign responsibilities, and manage deadlines. Entrepreneurs like Marie Forleo emphasize the importance of organizing both personal and professional tasks to maintain focus and productivity (Forleo 2019).

Enhance efficiency by streamlining processes to reduce waste and improve productivity. Tim Ferriss, author of *The 4-Hour Workweek,* advocates optimizing workflows through automation and delegation, allowing individuals to focus on high-impact tasks (Ferriss 2007). In business, Toyota's lean manufacturing principles have revolutionized production by eliminating inefficiencies and maximizing output (Liker 2004).

Plan effectively by setting clear goals and creating step-by-step plans to achieve them. Oprah Winfrey's success is partly due to her ability to envision long-term goals and break them into actionable steps (Kelley 2010). Similarly, Elon Musk's detailed planning process ensures that ambitious projects, like SpaceX's reusable rockets, are completed within tight schedules (Vance 2015).

Focus on execution by taking consistent action and paying attention to detail. Execution Geniuses understand that a well-thought-out plan is meaningless without proper implementation. Jeff Bezos built Amazon's success by ensuring that strategic initiatives were executed with precision, from optimizing supply chains to enhancing customer experiences (Stone 2013).

Leverage data to measure performance, identify trends, and make informed decisions. Netflix, for example, uses viewer data to guide content creation, ensuring that its shows and movies resonate with audiences (Smith 2016). Data-driven decisions have also propelled companies like Google, which uses analytics to optimize everything from search algorithms to workplace productivity (Schmidt & Rosenberg 2014).

Improve time management by prioritizing tasks based on importance and deadlines. Successful individuals like Richard Branson attribute their productivity to effective time management, using tools like calendars and to-do lists to stay organized (Branson 2006). In the entertainment industry, directors like James Cameron manage tight production schedules by carefully allocating time to each phase of filmmaking (Keegan 2009).

Build accountability by taking ownership of your work and ensuring that others do the same. Accountability is crucial for maintaining high standards and achieving long-term success. Teams at SpaceX are known for their culture of accountability, where each member is responsible for delivering high-quality results (Vance 2015).

By following these practical steps, individuals can develop their Execution Genius and achieve greater efficiency, productivity, and success in their personal and professional lives.

Development Strategy	Description
Master Organization	Use tools and systems to keep tasks structured and information accessible.
Enhance Efficiency	Streamline processes to reduce waste and improve productivity.
Plan Effectively	Set clear goals and create step-by-step plans to achieve them.
Focus on Execution	Implement plans with consistency and attention to detail.
Leverage Data	Use analytics to measure performance and guide decisions.
Improve Time Management	Prioritize tasks and manage time effectively to meet deadlines.
Build Accountability	Take ownership of your work and ensure that others do the same.

Achieving Operational Excellence

Execution Geniuses ensure that organizations operate efficiently and achieve their goals. Their ability to plan, organize, and execute complex tasks with precision makes them invaluable in fields ranging from business and engineering to entertainment and military operations. By developing their strengths and honing their skills, individuals can enhance their ability to optimize processes, make data-driven decisions, and deliver exceptional results in any professional setting.

Chapter References

Beyer, Kurt W. *Grace Hopper and the Invention of the Information Age.* MIT Press, 2009.

Blakely, Sara. *The Spanx Story: How Sara Blakely Turned $5,000 into a Billion-Dollar Business.* Entrepreneur Press, 2012.

Branson, Richard. *Screw It, Let's Do It: Lessons in Life.* Virgin Books, 2006.

Bundles, A'Lelia. *On Her Own Ground: The Life and Times of Madam C. J. Walker.* Scribner, 2001.

Clark, Duncan. *Alibaba: The House That Jack Ma Built.* Harper Business, 2016.

Clinton, Catherine. *Harriet Tubman: The Road to Freedom.* Little, Brown, 2004.

Davis, Benjamin O. *Benjamin O. Davis, Jr.: American.* Smithsonian Institution Press, 1991.

Drucker, Peter F. *Management Challenges for the 21st Century.* Harper Business, 1999.

Ferriss, Timothy. *The 4-Hour Workweek.* Crown Publishing Group, 2007.

Forleo, Marie. *Everything Is Figureoutable.* Portfolio, 2019.

Haber, Louis. *Black Pioneers of Science and Invention.* Harcourt, 1991.

Isaacson, Walter. *Steve Jobs.* Simon & Schuster, 2011.

Keegan, Rebecca. *James Cameron: Interviews.* University Press of Mississippi, 2009.

Kelley, Kitty. *Oprah: A Biography.* Crown Archetype, 2010.

Kirkpatrick, David. *The Facebook Effect: The Inside Story of the Company That Is Connecting the World.* Simon & Schuster, 2010.

Lemke, Kay. *Mary T. Washington Wylie: America's First Black Woman CPA.* NABA Publishing, 1994.

Liker, Jeffrey K. *The Toyota Way: 14 Management Principles from the World's Greatest Manufacturer.* McGraw-Hill, 2004. Morris, Bernice J. *Maggie Lena Walker and the Independent Order of St. Luke.* University of Virginia Press, 2003.

Passman, Donald S. *All You Need to Know About the Music Business.* 9th ed. Simon & Schuster, 2015.

Perkins, Melanie. *The Canva Story. Canva Blog*, 2021. https://www.canva.com/newsroom/

Robinson, Todd. *Christopher Nolan: A Critical Study of the Films.* McFarland, 2014.

Rogers, Naomi A. *Charles Drew: Doctor Who Got the World Pumped Up to Give Blood.* Enslow Publishers, 2013.

Schmidt, Eric, and Jonathan Rosenberg. *How Google Works.* Grand Central Publishing, 2014.

Schultz, Howard, and Dori J. Yang. *Onward: How Starbucks Fought for Its Life Without Losing Its Soul.* Rodale, 2011.

Shetterly, Margot Lee. *Hidden Figures: The American Dream and the Untold Story of the Black Women Mathematicians Who Helped Win the Space Race.* William Morrow, 2016.

Smith, Mark. *Netflix and the Culture of Reinvention.* Harvard Business Review Press, 2016.

Stone, Brad. *The Everything Store: Jeff Bezos and the Age of Amazon.* Little, Brown, 2013.

U.S. Department of Energy. *Frederick McKinley Jones: A Cooling Pioneer.* 2016. https://energy.gov

Vance, Ashlee. *Elon Musk: Tesla, SpaceX, and the Quest for a Fantastic Future.* HarperCollins, 2015.

Yousafzai, Malala, and Christina Lamb. *I Am Malala: The Girl Who Stood Up for Education and Was Shot by the Taliban.* Little, Brown and Company, 2013.

This page intentionally left blank

Chapter 5

The Power of CREATIVE GENIUS

Defining Creative Genius

Creative Geniuses possess an extraordinary ability to generate original ideas, tell compelling stories, and evoke emotions through their work. Their talent lies in transforming abstract concepts into tangible artistic expressions that captivate and inspire. This form of genius is essential in fields that involve self-expression, design, and emotional impact, such as music, writing, filmmaking, painting, graphic design, architecture, and fashion (Runco & Jaeger 2012).

Creativity manifests in both grand and subtle ways. A musician composing a melody that resonates with millions, a writer crafting characters that feel like old friends, and a filmmaker capturing moments that linger in memory all showcase Creative Genius. Consider Maya Angelou (Angelou 1969), whose poetry and prose conveyed profound emotions and advocated for social justice. On the other hand, Steve Jobs transformed everyday experiences with his innovative approach to design and technology (Isaacson 2011). Their work illustrates how creativity can bridge the gap between imagination and reality.

The essence of Creative Genius lies in perceiving the world differently and translating that vision into relatable, tangible forms. Filmmaker Ava DuVernay uses cinema to tell stories that challenge societal norms and spark dialogue (DuVernay 2016). Fashion designer Virgil Abloh redefined streetwear by merging it with high fashion, reshaping contemporary culture (Fury 2021). Their works captivate the senses while conveying messages that resonate with global audiences.

Creative Genius is about more than talent. It's about the courage to share one's unique perspective. It requires vulnerability, resilience, and a willingness to experiment. By exploring their emotions, experiences, and imagination, Creative Geniuses create works that connect with people on an intimately personal level, leaving a lasting impact that transcends time and place.

Core Strengths of Creative Geniuses

Creative Geniuses excel in several key areas that enable them to bring their ideas to life. These strengths are often showcased through real-world examples of individuals who have used their creativity to make a lasting impact.

Self-expression is essential for conveying emotions and personal experiences. Frida Kahlo's paintings explore themes of identity, pain, and resilience, resonating with audiences because of their raw honesty (Herrera 2002). Her work is a testament to the power of art as a means of self-exploration and communication. Similarly, musician Billie Eilish uses her music to express vulnerability and authenticity, creating songs that touch listeners worldwide (Eilish & O'Connell 2019).

Originality involves generating unique ideas that stand out from the crowd. Lin-Manuel Miranda reimagined American history through hip-hop in the musical *Hamilton*, creating a groundbreaking theatrical experience that captivated diverse audiences (Miranda 2015). His ability to blend historical narratives with contemporary music illustrates the power of innovation in storytelling. Likewise, fashion designer Alexander McQueen pushed the boundaries of fashion by merging avant-garde aesthetics with raw emotion (Bolton 2011).

Storytelling is about using narrative to engage and inspire. Chimamanda Ngozi Adichie's novels, such as *Half of a Yellow Sun,* bring complex cultural and historical issues to life, fostering empathy and understanding (Adichie 2006). In filmmaking, Christopher Nolan's intricate narratives and visual storytelling create immersive cinematic experiences that challenge audiences' perceptions (Robinson 2014).

Design is crucial for creating visually compelling works. Architect Zaha Hadid's futuristic buildings challenge conventional design, blending form and function with artistic flair (Zardini 2000). Graphic designer Paula Scher's bold and innovative typography has shaped the visual language of modern branding, proving that design can be both functional and expressive (Heller & Scher 2008).

Emotional impact is what makes art memorable. Photographer Gordon Parks used his camera to highlight social injustices, evoking empathy and driving change (Parks 1956). In dance, choreographer Alvin Ailey used movement to convey the African American experience, creating works that continue to inspire and educate audiences worldwide (DeFrantz 2004).

Core Strength	Description
Self-Expression	Conveying emotions and personal experiences through artistic mediums.
Originality	Generating unique ideas that capture attention and imagination.
Storytelling	Using narrative to engage, inspire, and connect with audiences.
Design	Creating visually compelling and aesthetically pleasing works.
Emotional Impact	Evoking emotions that leave a lasting impression.

Natural Aptitudes of Creative Geniuses

Creative Geniuses possess inherent qualities that enable them to excel in artistic and innovative roles. These natural aptitudes are often the driving force behind their ability to create work that resonates with others. This section thoroughly explores each aptitude, providing practical examples of internationally known artists who embody these qualities.

Imagination is the ability to envision new possibilities and think beyond conventional boundaries. This aptitude allows Creative Geniuses to see the world in ways others might overlook. For example, Salvador Dalí's surrealist paintings, such as *The Persistence of Memory* (Descharnes & Néret 2001), challenged traditional perceptions of reality. J.K. Rowling imagined an entire world of magic that captivated readers across the globe (Fraser 2000). Their works demonstrate how imagination can transform the ordinary into the extraordinary.

Curiosity drives Creative Geniuses to explore new ideas, cultures, and experiences. This relentless quest for knowledge fuels creativity and leads to the discovery of unique perspectives. Pablo Picasso's curiosity led him to develop multiple artistic styles, from Cubism to neoclassicism, pushing the boundaries of visual art (Richardson 1991). Similarly, Maya Angelou's exploration of different cultures and life experiences informed her poetry and prose, allowing her to connect with diverse audiences (Angelou 1986).

Sensitivity is a heightened awareness of one's own and others' emotions. This emotional depth enables artists to create work that profoundly connects with people. Vincent van Gogh's paintings, such as *Starry Night*, convey intense emotion through vibrant colors and expressive brushstrokes (Naifeh & Smith 2011). In music, Adele's soulful voice and heartfelt lyrics resonate with listeners worldwide, demonstrating how sensitivity can create a powerful emotional connection (Scobie 2016).

Risk-taking involves a willingness to experiment and challenge the status quo. Creative Geniuses are not afraid to push boundaries and explore unconven-tional ideas. Coco Chanel revolutionized fashion by introducing simple, elegant designs that challenged the restrictive styles of her time (Madsen 1990). In film, Alfred Hitchcock's innovative storytelling techniques, such as suspense and psychological tension, redefined the thriller genre in modern film (Truffaut 1984).

Resilience is the determination to overcome setbacks and continue creating. Success often requires perseverance in the face of criticism and failure. Ludwig van Beethoven continued to compose music despite losing his hearing, producing masterpieces such as *Symphony No. 9*

(Swafford 2014). Frida Kahlo transformed personal pain into compelling visual art, using her paintings to explore themes of identity and resilience (Herrera 2002).

These examples illustrate how the natural aptitudes of Creative Geniuses, imagination, curiosity, sensitivity, risk-taking, and resilience, enable them to create work that resonates with audiences worldwide.

Aptitude	Description
Imagination	Envisioning new possibilities beyond conventional boundaries.
Curiosity	Exploring new ideas, cultures, and experiences to fuel creativity.
Sensitivity	Creating emotionally resonant work through heightened awareness.
Risk-Taking	Challenging the status quo and experimenting with new techniques.
Resilience	Persevering through setbacks and continuing to create impactful work.

Common Professions and Applications

Creative Geniuses thrive in roles that require originality, storytelling, and emotional impact. Their ability to bring ideas to life is essential across various industries. For example, musicians like Yo-Yo Ma use their talent to evoke emotions and connect with audiences worldwide (Ma 2018), while writers like Haruki Murakami craft stories that blend the ordinary with the surreal (Rubin 2002), captivating readers with their unique perspectives. Filmmakers like Bong Joon-ho use visual storytelling to explore complex social issues, creating films that speak to audiences across cultures (Lee 2020). Painters like Yayoi Kusama express emotions and ideas through immersive visual art, using patterns and colors to evoke wonder and introspection (Munroe 2012).

Graphic designers like Paula Scher communicate powerful messages through innovative branding and design (Heller & Scher 2008), while architects like Frank Gehry combine aesthetics, functionality, and innovation to create iconic buildings that shape cityscapes (Jodidio 2009). Advertising executives like David Ogilvy develop campaigns that capture public attention and influence consumer behavior (Ogilvy 1985), while fashion designers such as Rei Kawakubo challenge traditional notions of clothing, creating garments that double as works of art (Bolton 2017).

Game designers like Hideo Kojima design immersive experiences that engage players' imaginations, blending narrative and gameplay to create powerfully emotional and intellectually stimulating journeys (Kent 2001). Photographers like Annie Leibovitz capture moments that tell stories and evoke emotions (Leibovitz 2008), while choreographers such as Pina Bausch use dance to convey complex narratives and explore the depths of human emotion (Hoghe 2008).

Profession	Application
Musicians	Composing music that evokes emotions and connects with audiences.
Writers	Crafting stories that entertain, inform, and inspire.
Filmmakers	Creating films that convey powerful narratives and visual experiences.
Painters	Expressing emotions and ideas through visual art.
Graphic Designers	Communicating messages through visual design and branding.

Architects	Designing buildings that combine aesthetics, functionality, and innovation.
Advertising Executives	Developing creative campaigns that capture public attention.
Fashion Designers	Creating clothing that reflects culture, identity, and artistic vision.
Game Designers	Designing immersive experiences that engage players' imagination.
Photographers	Capturing moments that tell stories and evoke emotions.
Choreographers	Creating dance routines that convey emotion and storytelling.

Developing Your Creative Geniuss

Cultivating Creative Genius involves nurturing specific skills and adopting practical strategies. This section provides a comprehensive, step-by-step approach to unlocking creativity, with examples to ignite your creative passions.

Developing Creative Genius begins with embracing imagination, the foun-dation of all creative endeavors. Allowing yourself to dream and explore new ideas without judgment opens the door to innovative thinking. Visual artists like Salvador Dalí and writers like J.K. Rowling highlight the power of imagination, transforming abstract concepts into thought-provoking works that captivate audiences worldwide (Descharnes & Néret 2001; Fraser 2000).

Fostering curiosity is essential for expanding your creative perspective. You can enrich your creative process by seeking inspiration from diverse sources, such as art, nature, culture, and personal experiences. For example,

Pablo Picasso's curiosity about different artistic styles led to the development of Cubism (Richardson 1991), while Maya Angelou's exploration of global cultures informed her powerful storytelling (Angelou 1986).

Expressing emotions through artistic mediums enables you to create work that strikes a chord with others. Whether through music, visual art, or literature, conveying genuine emotions adds depth and authenticity to your creations. Vincent van Gogh's emotionally charged paintings, such as *Starry Night* (Naifeh & Smith 2011), and Adele's heartfelt music illustrate the profound impact of emotional expression (Scobie 2016).

Taking risks is crucial for pushing creative boundaries and discovering new possibilities. Challenging conventional thinking and experimenting with innovative techniques often leads to groundbreaking work. Key figures in fashion and film, Coco Chanel (Madsen 1990) and Alfred Hitchcock (Truffaut 1984), redefined their respective creative areas to revolutionize their eras.

Building resilience is essential for overcoming setbacks and maintaining creative momentum. Success often requires persistence in the face of criticism and failure. Ludwig van Beethoven continued to compose despite losing his hearing (Swafford 2014). Frida Kahlo transformed personal pain into visually poignant art, demonstrating the importance of resilience in the creative journey (Herrera 2002).

Mastering your craft through continuous practice and learning is key to refining your skills and bringing your creative vision to life. Dedication and discipline allow you to achieve greater precision and confidence in your work. Musicians like Yo-Yo Ma (Ma 2018), writers like Haruki Murakami (Rubin 2002), and architects like Zaha Hadid

(Zardini 2000) exemplify the results of years of dedicated practice and innovation.

Connecting with others through collaboration and shared experiences can significantly enhance your creative process. Engaging with fellow creatives provides new insights, fosters innovation, and expands your artistic perspective. For example, Lin-Manuel Miranda's collaboration with diverse artists contributed to the success of *Hamilton* (Miranda 2015), while Alvin Ailey's work with dancers from various backgrounds enriched his choreography (DeFrantz 2004).

By following these steps, individuals can unlock their creative potential, develop their unique voice, and create work that inspires and connects with others. Whether through music, writing, art, or design, nurturing your Creative Genius allows you to leave a lasting impact on the world.

Development Strategy	Description
Embrace Imagination	Explore new ideas without limitations.
Foster Curiosity	Seek inspiration from diverse sources.
Express Emotions	Convey feelings through artistic mediums.
Take Risks	Challenge conventional thinking and experiment with new techniques.
Build Resilience	Persist through setbacks and keep creating.
Master Your Craft	Continuously refine skills through practice and learning.
Connect with Others	Collaborate with fellow creatives to expand your perspective.

The Impact of Creative Genius

Creative Geniuses play a vital role in shaping culture and society. Their ability to generate original ideas, tell compelling stories, and evoke emotions through their work enriches our lives and inspires future generations. Individuals can harness their Creative Genius to leave a lasting impact on the world by developing their strengths and honing their skills. Whether through music, art, writing, or design, the contributions of Creative Geniuses remind us of the power of human imagination and the importance of self-expression.

Chapter References

Adichie, Chimamanda Ngozi. *Half of a Yellow Sun.* Knopf, 2006.

Angelou, Maya. *I Know Why the Caged Bird Sings.* Random House, 1969.

Angelou, Maya. *All God's Children Need Traveling Shoes.* Random House, 1986.

Bolton, Andrew. *Alexander McQueen: Savage Beauty.* Metropolitan Museum of Art, 2011.

Bolton, Andrew. *Rei Kawakubo/Comme des Garçons: Art of the In-Between.* Metropolitan Museum of Art, 2017.

DeFrantz, Thomas F. *Dancing Revelations: Alvin Ailey's Embodiment of African American Culture.* Oxford University Press, 2004.

Descharnes, Robert, and Gilles Néret. *Salvador Dalí: The Paintings.* Taschen, 2001.
DuVernay, Ava, director. 13th. Netflix, 2016.

Eilish, Billie, and Finneas O'Connell. *When We All Fall Asleep, Where Do We Go?* Darkroom/Interscope Records, 2019.

Fraser, Lindsey. J.*K. Rowling: The Wizard Behind Harry Potter.* Wiley, 2000.

Fury, Alexander. *Virgil Abloh: Figures of Speech.* DelMonico Books, 2021.

Gehry, Frank. *The Complete Works.* Taschen, 2009.

Heller, Steven, and Paula Scher. *Make It Bigger.* Princeton Architectural Press, 2008.

Herrera, Hayden. *Frida: A Biography of Frida Kahlo.* Harper Perennial, 2002.

Hitchcock, Alfred, and François Truffaut. *Hitchcock.* Simon & Schuster, 1984.

Hoghe, Raimund. *Pina Bausch: Dance Theater.* Editions L'Arche, 2008.

Isaacson, Walter. *Steve Jobs.* Simon & Schuster, 2011.

Jodidio, Philip. *Architecture Now! Frank Gehry.* Taschen, 2009.

Kent, Steven. *The Ultimate History of Video Games.* Three Rivers Press, 2001.

Lee, Bong. *Bong Joon Ho: Master of Suspense.* Korean Film Council, 2020.

Leibovitz, Annie. *At Work.* Random House, 2008.

Ma, Yo-Yo. *Beginner's Mind.* Harvard University Lecture Series, 2018.

Madsen, Axel. *Chanel: A Woman of Her Own.* Henry Holt, 1990.

Miranda, Lin-Manuel. *Hamilton: An American Musical.* 2015.

Munroe, Alexandra. *Yayoi Kusama: Infinity Mirrors.* Hirshhorn Museum, 2012.

Naifeh, Steven, and Gregory White Smith. *Van Gogh: The Life.* Random House, 2011.

Ogilvy, David. *Ogilvy on Advertising.* Crown Publishing, 1985.

Parks, Gordon. *A Choice of Weapons.* Viking Press, 1966.

Richardson, John. *A Life of Picasso: Volume I.* Random House, 1991.

Robinson, Todd. *Christopher Nolan: A Critical Study of the Films.* McFarland, 2014.

Rubin, Jay. *Haruki Murakami and the Music of Words.* Harvill Press, 2002.

Runco, Mark A., and Garrett J. Jaeger. "The Standard Definition of *Creativity.*" *Creativity Research Journal* 24, no. 1 (2012): 92–96.

Scobie, Claire. *Adele: The Biography.* HarperCollins, 2016.

Swafford, Jan. *Beethoven: Anguish and Triumph.* Houghton Mifflin Harcourt, 2014.

Zardini, Mirko. *Zaha Hadid: The Complete Buildings and Projects.* Rizzoli, 2000.

Chapter 6

The Power of
PHYSICAL GENIUS

Defining Physical Genius

Physical Geniuses possess exceptional abilities in kinesthetic intelligence, coordination, craftsmanship, and endurance (Gardner 1983). Their talents are evident in their mastery of fine motor skills, problem-solving through tactile manipulation, and their capacity to perform in high-stakes environments. These skills are essential in fields that require precision, strength, and quick decision-making, such as athletics, city planning, construction, and emergency response.

In professional sports, athletes like Patrick Mahomes and Simone Biles exemplify remarkable coordination, strength, and agility (Longman 2019; Shpigel 2020). Mahomes' diverse throwing mechanics and strategic decision-making on the football field illustrate both physical control and mental acumen. Biles' mastery of complex gymnastic routines showcases kinesthetic intelligence and spatial awareness. Builders and city planners, such as Frank Gehry and Jane Jacobs, exhibit Physical Genius through their ability to design and construct structures that are both functional and aesthetically pleasing (Jacobs 1961; Jodidio 2009). Their work requires a deep understanding of materials, spatial relationships, and the practical needs of urban environments.

Physical Genius manifests in diverse ways. Construction workers use their strength and craftsmanship to build skyscrapers and bridges, while emergency responders rely on endurance and quick reflexes to save lives in critical situations. Mechanics apply hands-on problem-solving to diagnose and repair complex machinery, ensuring transportation and infrastructure systems operate smoothly. Integrating physical skills and intellectual problem-solving is essential to achieving excellence in these fields.

Core Strengths of Physical Geniuses

Physical Geniuses excel in several key areas that enable them to perform at the highest levels, often demonstrated through the accomplishments of individuals across diverse fields. Their core strengths include kinesthetic intelligence, coordination, craftsmanship, endurance, and hands-on problem-solving, each illustrated by real-world examples.

Kinesthetic intelligence is the ability to control bodily movements with precision, a skill essential for athletes, dancers, and martial artists. Simone Biles exemplifies this strength, executing complex gymnastic routines with remarkable accuracy and grace (Shpigel 2020). Bruce Lee portrayed kinesthetic intelligence through martial arts, combining speed, strength, and technique to revolutionize combat sports (Little 1997). Dancers like Misty Copeland showcase this ability through fluid, expressive movements that convey emotion and storytelling (Copeland 2014).

Coordination involves synchronizing different body parts to perform complex movements and fine motor skills. Michael Jordan's legendary basketball career highlights his exceptional coordination, allowing him to navigate defenders, execute precise shots, and perform gravity-defying dunks (Lazenby 2014). Surgeons like Dr. Ben Carson, renowned for pioneering neurosurgical procedures, rely on hand-eye coordination to perform delicate operations requiring both accuracy and control (Carson 1992).

Craftsmanship is the mastery of tools and materials, enabling artisans and mechanics to create and repair with exceptional skill. Henry Ford's innovations in automotive manufacturing transformed transportation, showcasing craftsmanship in both design and production (Watts 2005). Sculptors like Auguste Rodin used their hands to shape raw materials into timeless works of art. Meanwhile, carpenters and builders, such as those who constructed iconic skyscrapers like the Empire State Building, accentuate craftsmanship on a grand scale (Elsen 2003).

Endurance refers to sustained physical performance under demanding conditions. Usain Bolt's record-breaking sprinting achievements define endurance and speed, pushing the limits of human capability (Layden 2016). Firefighters rely on physical endurance to perform rescues in hazardous environments, such as those who responded during the 9/11 attacks (Kean & Hamilton 2004). Athletes like Serena Williams maintain their strength and stamina through rigorous training, enabling them to compete at the highest levels (Crouse 2019).

Hands-on problem-solving involves using tactile skills to diagnose and resolve issues in many areas, such as machinery, construction, or surgery. Steve Jobs ed this strength by physically interacting with prototypes to refine Apple's products, ensuring both functionality and aesthetic appeal (Isaacson 2011). Mechanics like those who maintain Formula 1 race cars use hands-on problem-solving to optimize performance under intense pressure (Saward 2005). Construction workers apply this skill to build an infrastructure that withstands the elements, ensuring safety and durability.

These examples highlight how the core strengths of Physical Geniuses, kinesthetic intelligence, coordination, craftsmanship, endurance, and hands-on problem-solving, enable individuals to excel in diverse fields, from sports and dance to construction and emergency response. Physical Geniuses possess innate qualities that empower them to excel in demanding environments.

Core Strength	Description
Kinesthetic Intelligence	Precise control of bodily movements for performance and creativity.
Coordination	Synchronization of body parts for complex and fluid movements.
Craftsmanship	Skilled use of tools and materials for creation and repair.
Endurance	Sustained physical performance under demanding conditions.
Hands-On Problem-Solving	Using tactile manipulation to diagnose and fix practical problems.

Natural Aptitudes of Physical Geniuses

Physical Geniuses possess innate qualities that enable them to excel in demanding environments. These natural aptitudes are exhibited through real-world examples from education, business, entertainment, and sports.

Dexterity refers to skillfully using hands and fingers for fine motor tasks. Surgeons like Dr. Ben Carson (Carson 1992) perform intricate procedures requiring steady hands and precise movements, while chefs like Gordon Ramsay use their dexterity to create culinary masterpieces (Ramsay 2006).

Strength and stamina are essential for prolonged physical activity. Athletes like LeBron James maintain peak performance through rigorous training (Windhorst 2020), and firefighters rely on physical strength to perform rescues in hazardous conditions (Kean & Hamilton 2004).

Spatial awareness involves understanding how the body moves in space. Dancers like Misty Copeland use spatial awareness to execute complex routines with grace and accuracy (Copeland 2014). Architects like Frank Lloyd Wright apply spatial awareness to design buildings that harmonize with their surroundings (Huxtable 2004).

Precision is crucial for accuracy in movement and execution. Baseball players like Derek Jeter embody precision when fielding and throwing (Verducci 2014), while craftsmen like Auguste Rodin use precise hand movements to sculpt detailed works of art (Elsen 2003).

Quick reflexes allow individuals to respond rapidly to stimuli, making split-second decisions under pressure. Emergency responders, such as paramedics and firefighters, rely on lightning-fast reflexes to assess and act in life-threatening situations. Athletes like Usain Bolt exhibit swift reflexes during sprinting competitions, allowing them to react instantly to the starting signal (Layden 2016; Kean & Hamilton 2004).

These natural aptitudes, dexterity, strength and stamina, spatial awareness, precision, and quick reflexes, are essential for success in fields that require physical skill, coordination, and quick thinking. They propel individuals to excel in diverse environments, from sports and entertainment to business and emergency response.

Aptitude	Description
Dexterity	Skilled use of hands and fingers is required for fine motor tasks.
Strength and Stamina	Physical power and endurance are necessary for prolonged activity.
Spatial Awareness	Understanding how the body moves in space is crucial for athletes and dancers.
Precision	Accuracy in movement and execution is essential for surgeons and craftsmen.
Quick Reflexes	Rapid response to stimuli enables split-second decisions.

Common Professions and Applications

Physical Geniuses thrive in professions that demand physical skill, coordination, and acute thinking. Their achievements have inspired nations and left a lasting impact across sports, arts, and essential services.

Athletes like Muhammad Ali transcended the boxing world with his unparalleled combination of speed, strength, and strategy (Hauser 1991). His Physical Genius extended beyond the ring, inspiring people worldwide through his resilience and charisma. Similarly, gymnast Nadia Comăneci became a global icon after scoring the first perfect 10 in Olympic history, showcasing extraordinary kinesthetic intelligence and grace (Llewellyn 2004).

Dancers like Mikhail Baryshnikov captivated audiences

with precision, fluidity, and emotional expression (Acocella 2007). His mastery of ballet and contemporary dance redefined physical storytelling. Meanwhile, Venus Williams broke barriers in tennis, eventually paving the way for her sister, Serena, to dominate the world of tennis.

Mechanics like John Deere revolutionized agriculture with machinery that transformed farming practices, demonstrating hands-on problem-solving at an industrial scale (Petroski 2006). In construction, figures like Emily Roebling played a pivotal role in completing the Brooklyn Bridge, showcasing leadership and engineering prowess (McCullough 1972).

Surgeons like Dr. Ben Carson, known for pioneering neurosurgical procedures, exemplify the precision required to perform life-saving operations (Carson 1992). Similarly, despite facing racial barriers, Dr. Vivien Thomas made groundbreaking contributions to cardiac surgery, inspiring future generations of medical professionals (Thomas 1985).

Chefs like Julia Child introduced French cuisine to American households, combining dexterity and creativity to elevate cooking into an art form (Child 2006). Electricians like Nikola Tesla harnessed their craftsmanship to revolutionize modern electricity, leaving a legacy that powers the world (Cheney 2011).

Sculptors like Auguste Rodin transformed blocks of marble into lifelike masterpieces (Elsen 2003), while martial artists like Bruce Lee used their Physical Genius to popularize martial arts and promote the philosophy of mind-body harmony (Little 1997). Firefighters and emergency responders demonstrated exceptional endurance and quick reflexes during crises such as 9/11, risking their lives to save others (Kean & Hamilton 2004).

Personal trainers like Jack LaLanne, known as the "Godfather of Fitness," revolutionized the health and fitness industry by promoting physical well-being and inspiring people worldwide to adopt healthier lifestyles (Gjerde 2003).

Profession	Application
Athletes	Performing at high levels of physical competition.
Dancers	Expressing emotion and storytelling through movement.
Mechanics	Diagnosing and repairing complex machinery.
Carpenters	Building and crafting structures with precision.
Construction Workers	Constructing buildings and infrastructure with accuracy and strength.
Surgeons	Performing precise medical procedures that require steady hands.
Chefs	Creating culinary art through skilled preparation and presentation.
Electricians	Installing and repairing electrical systems with attention to detail.
Sculptors	Shaping materials into artistic forms using tools and techniques.
Martial Artists	Combining strength, strategy, and coordination for combat and discipline.
Firefighters	Responding to emergencies with physical strength and endurance.
Emergency Responders	Providing life-saving care and rapid decision-making in crises.
Personal Trainers	Helping others improve their physical fitness and performance.

Developing Your Physical Genius

Cultivating Physical Genius involves building specific skills and adopting practical strategies. The following steps provide a straightforward, step-by-step approach to success, illustrated with detailed examples of individuals who have mastered these techniques.

Enhancing coordination is crucial for anyone seeking to develop Physical Genius. People achieve this through activities that synchronize movement and control, such as dance, sports, or martial arts. For example, Alvin Ailey transformed dance with strength, grace, and form, transfixing audiences internationally and inspiring dance in the African-American tradition for generations. Similarly, Katherine Dunham's dance technique blends classical ballet with Afro-Caribbean movement and is still taught and respected in dance institutions worldwide.

Building strength and endurance is essential for sustained physical performance. Athletes like Usain Bolt and Serena Williams achieved success by engaging in rigorous training to increase stamina and muscle strength (Layden 2016; Crouse 2019). Bolt's intense sprinting work-outs enabled him to break world records, while Williams' strength and endurance allowed her to dominate tennis courts worldwide. Police officers, military personnel, and construction workers also rely on physical strength to perform their demanding tasks, often enduring long hours of strenuous activity.

Refining motor skills requires focusing on tasks that demand precision, such as playing musical instruments, performing surgery, or using specialized tools. Surgeons like Dr. Charles R. Drew, a pioneering African American surgeon in the 20th century, revolutionized blood banking and transfusion practices, laying the groundwork for modern blood donation systems.

Developing spatial awareness is vital for understanding how the body moves in space. Gymnasts like Gabby Douglas and architects like Frank Lloyd Wright exemplify this aptitude (Shpigel 2020; Huxtable 2004). Biles's ability to control her body during complex routines showcases her advanced spatial awareness, while Wright's architectural designs demonstrate an understanding of spatial relationships that harmonize with their surroundings.

Strengthening reflexes is essential for responding swiftly to challenges. Quick decision-making can mean the difference between success and failure, whether on the basketball court or in high-stakes emergencies. Magic Johnson's ability to read the game in real time, anticipate plays, and react instantly was a key factor in his dominance as a point guard. Similarly, paramedics and emergency responders must assess situations rapidly, adapting on the spot to provide life-saving care. Just as Johnson later applied his strategic thinking and leadership to business, emergency professionals can harness their reflex-driven problem-solving skills in other areas of life, proving that sharp instincts and adaptability extend far beyond their primary roles.

Practicing problem-solving through hands-on projects helps develop tactile manipulation and creativity. Innovators across disciplines transform the world by applying hands-on problem-solving: agricultural pioneers like John Deere reimagined farming through engineering breakthroughs, while artists like Auguste Rodin reshaped perception with sculptural mastery. Similarly, tradespeople like carpenters and electricians use technical expertise and creative thinking to build and maintain the essential frameworks of daily life.

Committing to continuous learning is essential for long-term success. Athletes, artisans, and professionals study new techniques and seek expert guidance to refine their skills. Personal trainers like Jack LaLanne dedicated their careers to promoting physical fitness and educating others on the importance of maintaining their health (Gjerde 2003).

Development Strategy	Description
Enhance Coordination	Practice activities that synchronize movement and control.
Build Strength and Endurance	Engage in physical training to increase stamina and strength.
Refine Motor Skills	Focus on precise tasks that require dexterity and control.
Develop Spatial Awareness	Improve body awareness through activities like yoga and gymnastics.
Strengthen Reflexes	Train for quick reactions and decision-making in high-stakes situations.
Practice Problem-Solving	Use hands-on projects to enhance tactile manipulation and creativity.
Commit to Continuous Learning	Study new techniques and learn from experienced professionals.

The Power of Physical Mastery

Physical Geniuses play a vital role in shaping our world through their mastery of movement, craftsmanship, and problem-solving. Their ability to control their bodies with precision, endurance, and creativity allows them to excel in fields extending across sports and dance to surgery and construction. By developing these skills, individuals can unlock their physical potential, achieve exceptional results, and leave a lasting impact on the world around them.

Chapter References

Accocella, Joan. *Twenty-eight Artists and Two Saints: Essays.* Pantheon, 2007.

Carson, Ben. *Gifted Hands: The Ben Carson Story.* Zondervan, 1992.

Cheney, Margaret. *Tesla: Man Out of Time.* Simon & Schuster, 2011.

Child, Julia. *My Life in France.* Knopf, 2006.

Copeland, Misty. *Life in Motion: An Unlikely Ballerina.* Touchstone, 2014.

Crouse, Karen. S*erving Herself: The Life and Times of Serena Williams.* Farrar, Straus, and Giroux, 2019.

Elsen, Albert E. *Rodin.* Museum of Modern Art, 2003.

Gardner, Howard. *Frames of Mind: The Theory of Multiple Intelligences.* Basic Books, 1983.

Gjerde, Mark. *Jack LaLanne: Revolutionary Fitness Legend.* Fitness Press, 2003.

Hauser, Thomas. *Muhammad Ali: His Life and Times.* Simon & Schuster, 1991.

Huxtable, Ada Louise. *Frank Lloyd Wright: A Life.* Penguin Books, 2004.

Isaacson, Walter. *Steve Jobs.* Simon & Schuster, 2011.

Jacobs, Jane. *The Death and Life of Great American Cities.* Random House, 1961.

Jodidio, Philip. *Architecture Now! Frank Gehry.* Taschen, 2009.

Kean, Thomas H., and Lee H. Hamilton. T*he 9/11 Commission Report: Final Report of the National Commission on Terrorist Attacks Upon the United States.*
W. W. Norton & Company, 2004.

Lazenby, Roland. *Michael Jordan: The Life.* Little, Brown, 2014.

Layden, Tim. *Usain Bolt: The Fastest Man Alive.* Sports Illustrated Books, 2016.

Little, John. *Bruce Lee: A Life.* Tuttle Publishing, 1997.

Llewellyn, Marc. *Nadia Comăneci: Perfect Ten.* Lerner Publications, 2004.

McCullough, David. *The Great Bridge: The Epic Story of the Building of the Brooklyn Bridge.* Simon & Schuster, 1972.

Petroski, Henry. *The Essential Engineer: Why Science Alone Will Not Solve Our Global Problems.* Knopf, 2006.

Ramsay, Gordon. *Gordon Ramsay's Fast Food.* HarperCollins, 2006.

Saward, Joe. *The Grand Prix Saboteurs.* Motorbooks, 2005.

Shpigel, Ben. "Simone Biles Is the Best Gymnast Ever." *The New York Times*, February 18, 2020. https://nytimes.com

Thomas, Vivien. *Partners of the Heart.* University of Pennsylvania Press, 1985.

Verducci, Tom. *The Captain: The Journey of Derek Jeter.* Penguin Press, 2014.

Watts, Steven. *The People's Tycoon: Henry Ford and the American Century.* Knopf, 2005.

Windhorst, Brian. *LeBron, Inc.: The Making of a Billion-Dollar Athlete.* St. Martin's Press, 2020.

Chapter 7

Time to Find Your Genius (YES, YOU!)

Now that we have thoroughly explored all five types of natural genius, Visionary Genius, Relational Genius, Execution Genius, Creative Genius, and Physical Genius, it is time to reflect on which type resonates most with you. Each genius type offers a distinct set of strengths that can shape your path to success, whether through excelling in strategic thinking (Gardner 1983), forming meaningful connections (Goleman 2006), mastering efficiency (Covey 1989), creating art (Runco & Jaeger 2012), or achieving physical excellence (Ratey & Hagerman 2008).

Identifying your dominant genius can provide clarity about your natural talents, helping you make more confident decisions in both your personal and professional life. Understanding your strengths allows you to leverage them in ways that align with your passions and goals, ultimately unlocking your full potential (Clifton & Harter 2003). Whether you aspire to lead innovative projects, inspire others through your emotional intelligence, optimize processes for greater productivity, express yourself through art, or push the limits of physical performance, knowing your genius is the first step toward achieving your dreams.

Throughout history, individuals who recognized and harnessed their genius have made lasting impacts in their fields. Visionary leaders like Steve Jobs and Nelson Mandela transformed industries and societies through innovative thinking and strategic foresight (Isaacson 2011; Mandela 1995). Relational Geniuses like Rihanna and Martin Luther King Jr. connected with people on a profound level, inspiring movements and fostering change (Carson 1998). Rihanna revolutionized the beauty and fashion industries through her brand Fenty Beauty, celebrated for its inclusivity across skin tones, and became a billionaire by blending cultural influence with business innovation (Forbes 2021).

Execution Geniuses like Sheryl Sandberg and Tim Cook streamlined operations and built thriving organizations (Sandberg 2013; Lashinsky 2012). Creative Geniuses like Cindy Sherman and Lin-Manuel Miranda used their artistic talents to evoke emotions and tell compelling stories (Grundberg 1993; Miranda 2015). Cindy Sherman's groundbreaking use of photography to construct fictional identities revolutionized contemporary art and profoundly influenced cultural conversations around gender, media representation, and the performative nature of identity in late 20th-century and early 21st-century society (Grundberg 1993; Miranda 2015). Physical Geniuses like Serena Williams and Bruce Lee mastered their bodies to achieve feats of strength, agility, and endurance that captivated the world (Crouse 2019; Little 1997).

Now, it is your turn to discover the genius within you. The Genius Survey is designed to help you identify your dominant genius by assessing your natural inclinations, preferences, and strengths. By answering a series of thought-provoking questions, you will gain insights into which type of genius best represents your unique abilities. This knowledge can serve as a foundation for personal growth (Dweck 2006), guiding you toward opportunities that align with your talents and passions.

Imagine the possibilities that await once you understand your genius. If you are a Visionary Genius, you may find yourself leading innovative projects that shape the future. As a Relational Genius, you have the power to build meaningful relationships and inspire others to reach their full potential. If you are an Execution Genius, your ability to organize and optimize processes can drive success in any endeavor. As a Creative Genius, your artistic talents can bring beauty and meaning to the world. Additionally, if you are a Physical Genius, your mastery of movement and coordination can lead to achieve-ments in sports, performance, or craftsmanship.

Taking the Genius Survey is not just about identifying your dominant genius. It is about unlocking the potential within you and gaining the confidence to pursue your goals with passion and purpose. The survey results can provide valuable insights into how you think, feel, and act, empowering you to make choices that align with your true self. Whether seeking to advance your career, improve your relationships, or gain a more comprehensive understanding of yourself, discovering your genius is the key to living a more fulfilling and successful life.

So, are you ready to take the next step on your journey to greatness? Embrace the opportunity to uncover your unique strengths and unlock your full potential. Take the Genius Survey today and discover which type of genius defines you. Your journey toward personal and professional growth begins now.

The Natural Genius Survey: What's Your Genius?

Instructions: Rate each statement from 1 (nothing like me) to 5 (exactly like me).

#	Statement	1	2	3	4	5
1	I am highly organized and enjoy structuring processes.					
2	I feel energized by physical activity and movement.					
3	I love expressing myself through visual, musical, or written arts.					
4	I excel in sports, fitness, or activities requiring coordination.					
5	I enjoy learning by doing, working with my hands or body.					
6	I like solving real-world problems with hands-on approaches.					
7	I can visualize and bring artistic ideas to life.					
8	I easily build relationships and navigate social situations.					
9	I constantly think of new ideas and creative solutions.					
10	I naturally anticipate future trends and think long-term.					

#	Statement	1	2	3	4	5
11	I analyze information deeply before making decisions.					
12	I thrive in brainstorming sessions and love innovation.					
13	I enjoy making things run smoothly and eliminating inefficiencies.					
14	I perform well under physical pressure or time-sensitive conditions.					
15	I can quickly see the best path to success in complex situations.					
16	I often see possibilities where others see obstacles.					
17	I feel connected to my body and learn best through physical interaction.					
18	I thrive in structured environments with clear goals.					
19	I can assess risks and opportunities quickly and accurately.					
20	I prefer data-driven conclusions over gut feelings.					
21	I enjoy experimenting with new styles, colors, or forms of expression.					

#	Statement	1	2	3	4	5
22	I often seek deeper meaning and purpose in life.					
23	I can sense the emotions of others and respond appropriately.					
24	I am detail-oriented and enjoy executing well-planned tasks.					
25	I enjoy supporting others through challenges and celebrating their wins.					
26	I value harmony and collaboration in group settings.					
27	I often get "lost" in creative projects or artistic pursuits.					
28	I feel most myself when I'm making, designing, or storytelling.					
29	I use art, writing, or music to express things I can't say directly.					
30	People often come to me for emotional support or advice.					

The Five
NATURAL GENIUS
Types

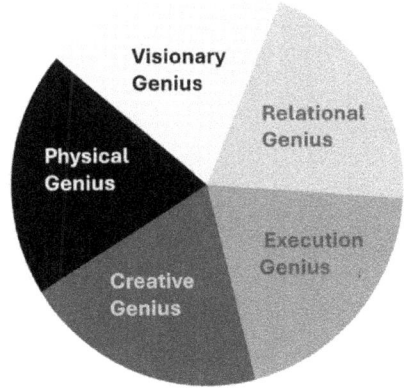

THE FIVE NATURAL GENIUS LEGEND

 => Visionary Genius

 => Relational Genius

 => Execution Genius

 => Creative Genius

 => Physical Genius

Scoring and Interpretation Table

Step 1: Add up your total score using the following chart.

Genius Type	Questions to Total	Your Score
Visionary Genius	9, 10, 12, 15, 16, 19	
Relational Genius	8, 22, 23, 25, 26, 30	
Execution Genius	1, 11, 13, 18, 20, 24	
Creative Genius	3, 7, 21, 27, 28, 29	
Physical Genius	2, 4, 5, 6, 14, 17	

Step 2: Identify your highest score. This represents your primary genius area. If you have a tie, you may possess a blend of two genius types!

Your Next Steps After Discovering Your Genius

Taking the Genius Survey is not just about identifying your dominant genius. It is about unlocking your potential and using that knowledge to drive real progress in your life. Now that you have discovered whether you are a Visionary Genius, Relational Genius, Execution Genius, Creative Genius, or Physical Genius, it is time to take action. Understanding your genius is the first step; applying it effectively will determine how far you can go. Whether you want to advance your career, improve your relationships, enhance your skills, or find an intensified sense of purpose, your genius can guide you toward success.

Aligning Your Genius with Your Goals

Now that you know your dominant genius, it's time to align it with your goals. Consider how you can leverage your genius in your career, personal life, and aspirations. If you are a Visionary Genius, you may want to explore leadership roles, entrepreneurship, or strategic problem-solving. If you are a Relational Genius, you might thrive in mentoring, counseling, or community-building roles. Execution Geniuses may find fulfillment in project management, business operations, or optimizing workflows. Creative Geniuses can excel in artistic expression, storytelling, and design, while Physical Geniuses should consider roles that involve movement, hands-on craftsmanship, or peak physical performance.

Applying Your Genius in Your Career

Your genius can be a game-changer in your professional life. Visionary Geniuses should seek roles that allow them to think big and create the future, such as business leadership, innovation, and strategic development. Relational Geniuses should gravitate toward positions where they can connect with and inspire people, such as coaching, teaching, and diplomacy. Execution Geniuses thrive in structured environments where efficiency is critical, making them perfect for operations management, finance, or business strategy roles. Creative Geniuses excel in any field requiring originality and artistic expression, including writing, filmmaking, music, and advertising. Physical Geniuses can pursue careers in sports, performance arts, emergency services, construction, or any field requiring hands-on problem-solving.

Strengthening Your Genius

Recognizing your genius is only the beginning. Now it's time to strengthen it. Here are practical steps you can take to develop your dominant genius further:

Visionary Geniuses: Read books on innovation and strategic thinking, practice brainstorming, and seek opportunities to lead projects that require long-term planning.

Relational Geniuses: Develop your emotional intelligence, practice active listening, and build strong networks to foster deeper connections.

Execution Geniuses: Improve your time management and organizational skills and seek ways to optimize efficiency in your school or workplace.

Creative Geniuses: Engage in regular creative exercises, explore different artistic mediums, and collaborate with other creatives to expand your perspectives.

Physical Geniuses: Maintain physical training, practice precision-based activities, and challenge yourself with new physical tasks to improve coordination and strength.

Seeking Mentorship and Inspiration

No matter what your genius is, learning from those who have mastered similar strengths can accelerate your growth. Seek out mentors, read about influential figures in your field, and surround yourself with people who complement and challenge your genius. If you are a Visionary Genius, study leaders like Tim Cook and Jeff Bezos (Lashinsky 2012; Stone 2013). Relational Geniuses can look to figures like Oprah Winfrey or Mahatma Gandhi (Winfrey 1998; Fischer 1982). Execution Geniuses should study great strategists and business leaders like Warren Buffett or Indra Nooyi (Buffett 2008; Nooyi 2021). Creative Geniuses can draw inspiration from artists like Vincent van Gogh or Maya Angelou (Naifeh & Smith 2011; Angelou 1969). Physical Geniuses can learn from athletes like Muhammad Ali or Bruce Lee (Hauser 1991; Little 1997).

Overcoming Challenges Based on Your Genius Type

Each type of genius comes with its own challenges. Recognizing these challenges can help you proactively work through them:

Visionary Geniuses may struggle with follow-through and must improve their ability to execute ideas.

Relational Geniuses sometimes prioritize others so much that they neglect their own goals.

Execution Geniuses can become overly rigid and struggle to adapt to creative or unstructured environments.

Creative Geniuses often face self-doubt or perfectionism that can hinder their progress.

Physical Geniuses might need to balance physical mastery with intellectual or emotional growth.

Expanding Your Genius Beyond Your Dominant Type

Even though you have a dominant genius, you are not limited to just one. Human potential is vast, and the most successful individuals recognize the value of expanding their abilities beyond their primary strengths. Developing complementary skills enhances their effectiveness, adaptability, and long-term success. A Visionary Genius, known for their big ideas and ability to see future possibilities, can improve their execution skills to bring their ideas to life in a tangible way. Without execution, even the most brilliant ideas remain just concepts. A Visionary Genius can transform dreams into reality by learning project management, time management, and implementation strategies. A Relational Genius, naturally gifted at building connections and fostering collaboration, can adopt strategic thinking to become a more effective leader. Strong interpersonal skills create trust and influence. They add a strategic mindset that equips a Relational Genius to navigate complex organizational challenges, make data-driven decisions, and set a clear direction for others. By mastering analytical thinking, decision-making frameworks, and problem-solving techniques, they can lead with both empathy and intelligence.

An Execution Genius, skilled at efficiency, precision, and getting things done, can develop creative skills to make their work more innovative. While their strength lies in discipline and structure, creativity allows them to adapt, think outside the box, and find novel solutions to problems. By engaging in brainstorming exercises, experimenting with different perspectives, and embracing flexibility, an Execution Genius can elevate their work from merely efficient to groundbreaking.

A Creative Genius, bursting with imagination, originality, and artistic vision, can benefit from learning structure and efficiency to become more productive. While creativity fuels innovation, discipline ensures that ideas turn into completed projects. A Creative Genius can maximize their impact and turn inspiration into tangible achievements by incorporating goal-setting, scheduling, and prioritization. Combining creativity with organization leads to sustained success rather than fleeting bursts of brilliance.

A Physical Genius, whose strengths lie in athleticism, movement, and kinesthetic intelligence, can deepen their understanding of strategy and teamwork to complement their physical mastery. While physical skill and endurance are essential, understanding game theory, leadership dynamics, and effective communication can take their abilities to the next level. By studying tactical approaches, learning from experienced mentors, and enhancing their ability to work within a team, a Physical Genius can transcend individual talent and contribute to collective success.

Individuals unlock their full potential and achieve remarkable success by expanding beyond their dominant genius and cultivating complementary skills. True mastery comes not from staying within one's comfort zone but from embracing growth and adaptability.

Creating a Personal Development Plan

To make the most of your genius, create a plan for growth:

1. **Set Goals:** Define what success looks like for you and how your genius can help you get there.

2. **Identify Strengths and Weaknesses:** Understand where you naturally excel and where you need to improve.

3. **Seek Out Opportunities:** Look for ways to use your genius in your career, hobbies, and relationships.

4. **Commit to Learning:** Take courses, read books, and find mentors to help you develop further.

5. **Measure Progress:** Regularly reflect on your growth and adjust your approach.

Personal Development Plan

1. Set Goals

What does success look like for you? How can your genius help you achieve it?

➡ _____

➡ _____

➡ _____

2. Identify Strengths and Weaknesses

Where do you naturally excel? Where do you need to improve?

✓ *Strengths:* _____

✓ *Weaknesses:* _____

3. Seek Out Opportunities

Where can you use your genius in your career, hobbies, and relationships?

✦ *Career:* _____

✦ *Hobbies:* _____

✦ *Relationships:* _____

4. Commit to Learning

What books, courses, or mentors can help you grow?

📖 *Books:* _____

🎓 *Courses:* _____

👤 *Mentors:* _____

5. Measure Progress

How will you track your growth and adjust as needed?

✅ *Reflection Notes:* _____

✅ *Adjsutments:* _____

The Next Chapter of Your Life

Your journey toward personal and professional growth starts now. Understan-ding your genius is not just about self-awareness, it's about using that knowledge to create a meaningful and fulfilling life. Whether you innovate, inspire, optimize, create, or perform, your genius is your superpower (Pink 2009). The Genius Survey was only the first step. Now, apply what you have learned to your life with confidence, curiosity, and purpose. Your genius is waiting to be unleashed. The next chapter of your life is yours to write.

Chapter References

Angelou, Maya. *I Know Why the Caged Bird Sings*. Random House, 1969.

Buffett, Warren. *The Essays of Warren Buffett: Lessons for Corporate America*. The Cunningham Group, 2008.

Carson, Clayborne. *The Autobiography of Martin Luther King, Jr.* Warner Books, 1998.

Christensen, Clayton M. *The Innovator's Dilemma: When New Technologies Cause Great Firms to Fail*. Harvard Business Review Press, 1997.

Clifton, Donald O., and James K. Harter. *StrengthsQuest: Discover and Develop Your Strengths in Academics, Career, and Beyond*. Gallup Press, 2003.

Covey, Stephen R. *The 7 Habits of Highly Effective People*. Free Press, 1989.

Crouse, Karen. *Serving Herself: The Life and Times of Serena Williams*. Farrar, Straus, and Giroux, 2019.

Duckworth, Angela. *Grit: The Power of Passion and Perseverance*. Scribner, 2016.

Dweck, Carol S. *Mindset: The New Psychology of Success*. Random House, 2006.

Fischer, Louis. *The Life of Mahatma Gandhi*. Harper & Row, 1982.

Gardner, Howard. F*rames of Mind: The Theory of Multiple Intelligences*. Basic Books, 1983.

Goleman, Daniel. *Emotional Intelligence: Why It Can Matter More Than IQ*. Bantam, 2006.

Hauser, Thomas. *Muhammad Ali: His Life and Times.* Simon & Schuster, 1991.

Herrera, Hayden. *Frida: A Biography of Frida Kahlo.* Harper Perennial, 2002.

Isaacson, Walter. *Steve Jobs.* Simon & Schuster, 2011.

Lashinsky, Adam. *Inside Apple: How America's Most Admired, and Secretive, Company Really Works.* Business Plus, 2012.

Little, John. *Bruce Lee: A Life.* Tuttle Publishing, 1997.

Mandela, Nelson. *Long Walk to Freedom: The Autobiography of Nelson Mandela.* Little, Brown, 1995.

Miranda, Lin-Manuel. *Hamilton: An American Musical.* 2015.

Naifeh, Steven, and Gregory White Smith. *Van Gogh: The Life.* Random House, 2011.

Nooyi, Indra. *My Life in Full: Work, Family, and Our Future.* Portfolio, 2021.

Pink, Daniel H. *Drive: The Surprising Truth About What Motivates Us.*
Riverhead Books, 2009.

Ratey, John J., and Eric Hagerman. Spark: The Revolutionary New Science of Exercise and the Brain. Little, Brown, 2008.

Runco, Mark A., and Garrett J. Jaeger. "The Standard Definition of Creativity." *Creativity Research Journal* 24, no. 1 (2012): 92–96.
https://doi.org/10.1080/10400419.2012.650092

Sandberg, Sheryl. *Lean In: Women, Work, and the Will to Lead.* Knopf, 2013.

Stone, Brad. *The Everything Store: Jeff Bezos and the Age of Amazon.* Little, Brown, 2013.

Winfrey, Oprah. *The Uncommon Wisdom of Oprah Winfrey: A Portrait in Her Own Words.* Carol Publishing Group, 1998.

ABOUT THE AUTHOR

Dr. Jason E. Gines

Cultural Thought Leader, Organizational Designer and Strategist, and Relational Genius

With over 15 years of experience leading transformative initiatives across complex organizations, I am Dr. Jason E. Gines, an accomplished executive leader recognized for shaping high-performance cultures and driving strategic growth. My expertise spans end-to-end program design, organizational design and development, executive leadership, and data-driven decision-making to optimize systems and accelerate results. Equipped with a Ph.D. and a career that bridges education, leadership consulting, and organizational strategy, I specialize in translating vision into measurable impact through actionable frameworks and sustainable solutions..

Proven Leadership in Complex Environments

I have successfully led enterprise-level initiatives that enhanced operational performance, aligned teams to shared goals, and cultivated environments where innovation thrives. My career includes designing large-scale strategic plans, managing multi-stakeholder projects, and guiding leaders through pivotal organizational change. Known for my ability to connect big-picture vision with practical execution, I have consistently delivered outcomes that strengthen systems, improve engagement, and create lasting impact.

A Scholarly and Practitioner-Based Perspective

My background as a former assistant professor and researcher brings a unique depth to my leadership practice. I have taught, mentored, and advised emerging leaders while conducting grant-funded research that bridges theory with application. My work has been featured in professional publications and conferences, underscoring my ability to synthesize complex ideas into practical strategies that drive individual and organizational success.

Why I Wrote the Book on Genius

Years of experience working with leaders, teams, and individuals revealed a truth: every person possesses a unique genius that, when identified and activated, can transform not only their own life but the organizations and communities they influence. My expertise across sectors, combined with my academic rigor and hands-on leadership, positions me uniquely to define, articulate, and guide others in discovering and applying their own natural genius.

Ready to Discover Your Natural Genius? Let's Thrive.

Connect with Jason's team via:

Website: www.GinesGlobalAdvisors.com

Email: jasonginesphd@gmail.com

Social:
FB: Jason.Gines | *LinkedIn:* linkedin.com/in/drjasongines/

Services: Speaking | Consultations | Events | Workshops

We are Activating 1M Genius' worldwide. Join Us. Share the Books.
High School Students, Graduates & Professionals: Unlock Tiered and Exclusive Access

Purchase 1 copy + *Join the Genius Nation* = Genius Badge

Purchase 3 copies *(1ea for a Peer, Advisor, and/Family Member)* =
1:1 Strategy Session with Dr. Jason E. Gines

Purchase 10 copies = Complimentary Virtual Genius Session w/ you, Group of 10 and Dr. Jason E. Gines

- **Groups & Organizations:** Discount Available for Bulk Orders

- 100+ Copies purchased includes a **Free Signing Session** with your group

- 1000+ Copies purchased includes a **Free ½ Day Workshop** with your group

INDEX

A

Adaptability, 42, 68
Aligning genius with goals, 100
Artistic expression, 66–67

C

Collaboration, 33, 36, 89
Communication,42, 67
Creative Genius, 65–78
Core Strengths, 66
Natural Aptitudes, 68–70
Common Professions, 70–71
Development Strategies, 72–74
Visual: Creative Genius Infographic, 65

D

Data-driven decisions, 52–53
Dexterity, 82–83
Diversity of genius, 98–99

E

Emotional Intelligence, 38–39,73
Execution Genius, 51–64
Core Strengths, 52
Natural Aptitudes, 54–55
Common Professions, 55–57
Development Strategies, 58–60
Visual: Execution Genius Infographic, 51

G

Genius Assessment, 95–97
Revised 30-question version, 96

Genius Expansion, 103–105
Genius Types Overview, 1–5
Goal setting, 101, 106

I
Imagination, 66–67
Index, 114–117
Innovation, 6, 13, 42, 65

L
Leadership, 9, 14, 39, 88

M
Mentorship, 102
Motor skills, 82–83
Movement, 79–81

P
Personal Development Plan, 106–107
Physical Genius, 79–92
Core Strengths, 82–83
Natural Aptitudes, 84–86
Common Professions, 87–89
Development Strategies, 79
Visual: Physical Genius Infographic, 70
Pie Chart of Genius Types, 95
Problem-solving, 52, 58, 82

R
Relational Genius, 37–50
Core Strengths, 38
Natural Aptitudes, 41–42
Common Professions, 43–45
Development Strategies, 46–48
Visual: Relational Genius Infographic, 37

S
Scoring Table, 97
Self-Discovery, 90–91
Spatial Awareness, 82–83

V
Visionary Genius, 21–36
Core Strengths, 22–24
Natural Aptitudes, 25–26
Common Professions, 27–30
Development Strategies, 31–33
Visual: Visionary Genius Infographic, 21
Visual: Genius Pie Chart, 95
Visual: Genius Pie Chart with Legend, 96

APPENDIX

Survey & Scoring Interpretation Table

Your journey toward personal and professional growth begins now.

The Natural Genius Survey: What's Your Genius?

Instructions: Rate each statement from 1 (nothing like me) to 5 (exactly like me).

#	Statement	1	2	3	4	5
1	I am highly organized and enjoy structuring processes.					
2	I feel energized by physical activity and movement.					
3	I love expressing myself through visual, musical, or written arts.					
4	I excel in sports, fitness, or activities requiring coordination.					
5	I enjoy learning by doing, working with my hands or body.					
6	I like solving real-world problems with hands-on approaches.					
7	I can visualize and bring artistic ideas to life.					
8	I easily build relationships and navigate social situations.					
9	I constantly think of new ideas and creative solutions.					
10	I naturally anticipate future trends and think long-term.					

#	Statement	1	2	3	4	5
11	I analyze information deeply before making decisions.					
12	I thrive in brainstorming sessions and love innovation.					
13	I enjoy making things run smoothly and eliminating inefficiencies.					
14	I perform well under physical pressure or time-sensitive conditions.					
15	I can quickly see the best path to success in complex situations.					
16	I often see possibilities where others see obstacles.					
17	I feel connected to my body and learn best through physical interaction.					
18	I thrive in structured environments with clear goals.					
19	I can assess risks and opportunities quickly and accurately.					
20	I prefer data-driven conclusions over gut feelings.					
21	I enjoy experimenting with new styles, colors, or forms of expression.					
22	I often seek deeper meaning and purpose in life.					
23	I can sense the emotions of others and respond appropriately.					
24	I am detail-oriented and enjoy executing well-planned tasks.					
25	I enjoy supporting others through challenges and celebrating their wins.					
26	I value harmony and collaboration in group settings.					

27	I often get "lost" in creative projects or artistic pursuits.					
28	I feel most myself when I'm making, designing, or storytelling.					
29	I use art, writing, or music to express things I can't say directly.					
30	People often come to me for emotional support or advice.					

The Five
NATURAL GENIUS
Types

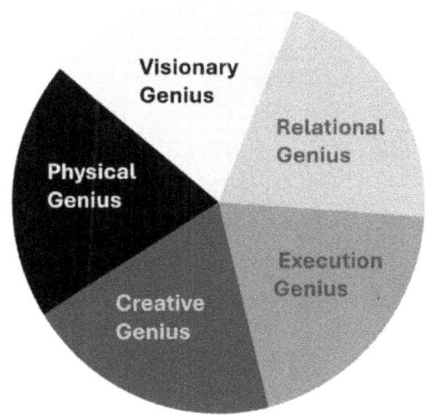

THE FIVE NATURAL GENIUS LEGEND

=> Visionary Genius

=> Relational Genius

=> Execution Genius

=> Creative Genius

=> Physical Genius

Tables for Core Strengths, Aptitudes, Professions and Development Strategy for each Genius

Visionary Genius

Core Strength	Description
Big-Picture Thinking	Ability to see the overarching context and long-term implications.
Innovation	Challenging the status quo and seeking creative solutions.
Strategic Problem-Solving	Analyzing trends to address current and future challenges.
Future-Oriented Mindset	Constantly anticipating emerging opportunities and potential threats.

Aptitude	Description
Curiosity	The constant drive to explore new ideas and knowledge.
Creativity	Thinking outside the box to generate innovative solutions.
Analytical Thinking	Breaking down complex problems into manageable components.
Empathy	Understanding and addressing the needs of others.
Resilience	Overcoming obstacles and maintaining determination.

Profession	Application
Entrepreneurs	Building innovative businesses that challenge traditional industries.
CEOs	Leading organizations with future-focused strategies.
Futurists	Analyzing and predicting trends to guide decision-making.
Inventors	Developing technologies that revolutionize everyday life.
Politicians	Crafting policies to address long-term societal challenges.
Business Strategists	Designing strategies that ensure sustainable growth.
Thought Leaders	Shaping public discourse and influencing societal values.
Research Scientists	Expanding human knowledge through pioneering discoveries.
Change Agents	Leading social movements that drive positive change.
Venture Capitalists	Investing in startups poised to reshape entire industries.

Development Strategy	Description
Expand Knowledge	Continuously explore diverse fields of study.
Think Long-Term	Focus on long-term impact rather than short-term gains.
Connect the Dots	Identify connections between seemingly unrelated ideas.
Embrace Creativity	Challenge conventional thinking to discover new solutions.
Develop Strategic Thinking	Analyze current trends to anticipate future developments.

| Build Resilience | Learn from setbacks and persist despite challenges. |
| Inspire Others | Communicate your vision to motivate and guide others. |

Relational Genius

Core Strength	Description
Emotional Intelligence	Understanding and managing one's emotions while recognizing and responding to the feelings of others.
Empathy	The ability to understand and share the feelings of others and foster compassion and trust.
Connection	Building authentic relationships and creating environments where people feel valued and understood.
Leadership	Guiding and inspiring others to achieve their goals and realize their potential.
Community Building	Creating a sense of belonging and shared purpose within groups and organizations.

Aptitude	Description
Active Listening	Fully engaging with others, demonstrating attentiveness and understanding.
Communication	Expressing ideas clearly and empathetically and fostering open dialogue.
Compassion	Showing genuine care and concern for the well-being of others.

| Adaptability | Adjusting one's approach to meet the needs of different individuals and situations. |
| Conflict Resolution | Mediating disputes and promoting harmony through understanding and compromise. |

Profession	Application
Therapists	Help individuals navigate emotional and psychological challenges.
Counselors	Provide support and guidance to individuals and families.
Teachers	Inspire and educate students, fostering both academic and personal growth.
Social Workers	Advocate for individuals and communities to improve their well-being.
Religious Leaders	Offer spiritual guidance and create supportive faith communities.
Coaches	Empower individuals to reach their personal and professional goals.
Human Resources Professionals	Build positive workplace cultures and support employee development.
Diplomats	Facilitate communication and cooperation between nations.
Customer Relations Managers	Ensure positive interactions between businesses and their customers.
Community Organizers	Lead social movements and foster collective action.
Conflict Mediators	Resolve disputes and promote understanding and collaboration.

Development Strategy	Description
Practice Active Listening	Focus on truly hearing and understanding what others are saying.
Enhance Emotional Intelligence	Develop awareness of your own emotions and learn to recognize and respond to the moods of others.
Build Authentic Connections	Foster genuine relationships based on trust, empathy, and mutual respect.
Improve Communication Skills	Learn to express your thoughts clearly and empathetically.
Cultivate Compassion	Approach others with kindness and a genuine desire to help.
Develop Conflict Resolution Skills	Learn techniques for resolving disputes and promoting understanding.
Lead with Empathy	Inspire and guide others by understanding their needs and motivations.

Execution Genius

Core Strength	Description
Organization	Structuring tasks and processes to maximize efficiency and productivity.
Efficiency	Using resources effectively to achieve goals with minimal waste.
Planning	Developing comprehensive strategies to achieve long-term objectives.
Execution	Implementing plans and ensuring that tasks are completed successfully.
Data-Driven Decision-Making	Using data and analytics to guide decisions and improve outcomes.

Aptitude	Description
Attention to Detail	Ensuring that every component of a project is accurate and precise.
Logical Thinking	Analyzing problems and developing practical solutions.
Time Management	Prioritizing tasks to meet deadlines without compromising quality.
Adaptability	Adjusting plans and strategies to address unexpected challenges.
Accountability	Taking responsibility for outcomes and ensuring that goals are met.

Profession	Application
Project Managers	Overseeing projects from initiation to completion, ensuring efficiency.
Engineers	Designing and implementing systems and structures.
Business Analysts	Analyzing data to improve business processes and decision-making.
Supply Chain Managers	Managing the flow of goods and services to ensure timely delivery.
Financial Analysts	Using data to guide investment and financial decisions.
Military Leaders	Coordinating complex operations and ensuring mission success.
Accountants	Maintaining financial accuracy and compliance.
Quality Control Experts	Ensuring that products meet industry standards and customer expectations.
Process Improvement Specialists	Identifying inefficiencies and optimizing workflows.
Logisticians	Managing transportation and distribution to ensure timely delivery.

Development Strategy	Description
Master Organization	Use tools and systems to keep tasks structured and information accessible.
Enhance Efficiency	Streamline processes to reduce waste and improve productivity.
Plan Effectively	Set clear goals and create step-by-step plans to achieve them.
Focus on Execution	Implement plans with consistency and attention to detail.

Leverage Data	Use analytics to measure performance and guide decisions.
Improve Time Management	Prioritize tasks and manage time effectively to meet deadlines.
Build Accountability	Take ownership of your work and ensure that others do the same.

Creative Genius

Core Strength	Description
Self-Expression	Conveying emotions and personal experiences through artistic mediums.
Originality	Generating unique ideas that capture attention and imagination.
Storytelling	Using narrative to engage, inspire, and connect with audiences.
Design	Creating visually compelling and aesthetically pleasing works.
Emotional Impact	Evoking emotions that leave a lasting impression.

Aptitude	Description	Example
Imagination	Envisioning new possibilities beyond conventional boundaries.	Salvador Dalí, J.K. Rowling
Curiosity	Exploring new ideas, cultures, and experiences to fuel creativity.	Pablo Picasso, Maya Angelou
Sensitivity	Creating emotionally resonant work through heightened awareness.	Vincent van Gogh, Adele

| Risk-Taking | Challenging the status quo and experimenting with new techniques. | Coco Chanel, Alfred Hitchcock |
| Resilience | Persevering through setbacks and continuing to create impactful work. | Ludwig van Beethoven, Frida Kahlo |

Profession	Application
Musicians	Composing music that evokes emotions and connects with audiences.
Writers	Crafting stories that entertain, inform, and inspire.
Filmmakers	Creating films that convey powerful narratives and visual experiences.
Painters	Expressing emotions and ideas through visual art.
Graphic Designers	Communicating messages through visual design and branding.
Architects	Designing buildings that combine aesthetics, functionality, and innovation.
Advertising Executives	Developing creative campaigns that capture public attention.
Fashion Designers	Creating clothing that reflects culture, identity, and artistic vision.
Game Designers	Designing immersive experiences that engage players' imagination.
Photographers	Capturing moments that tell stories and evoke emotions.
Choreographers	Creating dance routines that convey emotion and storytelling.

Development Strategy	Description
Embrace Imagination	Explore new ideas without limitations.
Foster Curiosity	Seek inspiration from diverse sources.
Express Emotions	Convey feelings through artistic mediums.
Take Risks	Challenge conventional thinking and experiment with new techniques.
Build Resilience	Persist through setbacks and keep creating.
Master Your Craft	Continuously refine skills through practice and learning.
Connect with Others	Collaborate with fellow creatives to expand your perspective.

Physical Genius

Core Strength	Description
Kinesthetic Intelligence	Precise control of bodily movements for performance and creativity.
Coordination	Synchronization of body parts for complex and fluid movements.
Craftsmanship	Skilled use of tools and materials for creation and repair.
Endurance	Sustained physical performance under demanding conditions.
Hands-On Problem-Solving	Using tactile manipulation to diagnose and fix practical problems.

Aptitude	Description
Dexterity	Skilled use of hands and fingers is required for fine motor tasks.
Strength and Stamina	Physical power and endurance are necessary for prolonged activity.
Spatial Awareness	Understanding how the body moves in space is crucial for athletes and dancers.
Precision	Accuracy in movement and execution is essential for surgeons and craftsmen.
Quick Reflexes	Rapid response to stimuli enables split-second decisions.

Profession	Application
Athletes	Performing at high levels of physical competition.
Dancers	Expressing emotion and storytelling through movement.
Mechanics	Diagnosing and repairing complex machinery.
Carpenters	Building and crafting structures with precision.
Construction Workers	Constructing buildings and infrastructure with accuracy and strength.
Surgeons	Performing precise medical procedures that require steady hands.
Chefs	Creating culinary art through skilled preparation and presentation.
Electricians	Installing and repairing electrical systems with attention to detail.
Sculptors	Shaping materials into artistic forms using tools and techniques.
Martial Artists	Combining strength, strategy, and coordination for combat and discipline.
Firefighters	Responding to emergencies with physical strength and endurance.
Emergency Responders	Providing life-saving care and rapid decision-making in crises.
Personal Trainers	Helping others improve their physical fitness and performance.

Development Strategy	Description
Enhance Coordination	Practice activities that synchronize movement and control.
Build Strength and Endurance	Engage in physical training to increase stamina and strength.
Refine Motor Skills	Focus on precise tasks that require dexterity and control.
Develop Spatial Awareness	Improve body awareness through activities like yoga and gymnastics.
Strengthen Reflexes	Train for quick reactions and decision-making in high-stakes situations.
Practice Problem-Solving	Use hands-on projects to enhance tactile manipulation and creativity.
Commit to Continuous Learning	Study new techniques and learn from experienced professionals.

REFERENCE LIST
(Alphabetized)

A

- Acocella, J. (2007). *Twenty-eight Artists and Two Saints: Essays.* Pantheon.
- Adichie, C. N. (2006). *Half of a Yellow Sun.* Knopf.
- Annan, K. (2012). *Interventions: A Life in War and Peace.* Penguin.
- Angelou, M. (1969). *I Know Why the Caged Bird Sings.* Random House.
- Angelou, M. (1986). *All God's Children Need Traveling Shoes.* Random House.

B

- Beyer, K. W. (2009). *Grace Hopper and the Invention of the Information Age.* MIT Press.
- Blakely, S. (2012). *The Spanx Story: How Sara Blakely Turned $5,000 into a Billion-Dollar Business.* Entrepreneur Press.
- Bolton, A. (2011). *Alexander McQueen: Savage Beauty.* Metropolitan Museum of Art.
- Bolton, A. (2017). *Rei Kawakubo/Comme des Garçons: Art of the In-Between.* Metropolitan Museum of Art.
- Branch, T. (1988). *Parting the Waters: America in the King Years* 1954-63. Simon & Schuster.
- Branson, R. (1998). *Losing My Virginity: How I Survived, Had Fun, and Made a Fortune Doing Business My Way.* Crown Publishing.
- Branson, R. (2006). *Screw It, Let's Do It: Lessons in Life.* Virgin Books.
- Brennan, C. (2020, June 4). LeBron James continues to show leadership off the court. *USA Today.* https://www.usatoday.com
- Bundles, A. L. (2001). *On Her Own Ground: The Life and Times of Madam C. J. Walker.* Scribner.

- Burns, U. (2021). *Where You Are Is Not Who You Are: A Memoir.* Amistad.
- Buffett, W. (2008). *The Essays of Warren Buffett: Lessons for Corporate America.* The Cunningham Group.

C
- Carson, B. (1992). *Gifted Hands: The Ben Carson Story.* Zondervan.
- Carson, C. (1998). *The Autobiography of Martin Luther King, Jr.* Warner Books.
- Child, J. (2006). *My Life in France.* Knopf.
- Cheney, M. (2011). *Tesla: Man Out of Time.* Simon & Schuster.
- Christensen, C. M. (1997). *The Innovator's Dilemma: When New Technologies*
- *Cause Great Firms to Fail.* Harvard Business Review Press.
- Clark, D. (2016). *Alibaba: The House That Jack Ma Built.* Harper Business.
- Clifton, D. O., & Harter, J. K. (2003). *StrengthsQuest: Discover and Develop Your Strengths in Academics, Career, and Beyond.* Gallup Press.
- Clinton, C. (2004). *Harriet Tubman: The Road to Freedom.* Little, Brown.
- Copeland, M. (2014). *Life in Motion: An Unlikely Ballerina.* Touchstone.
- Covey, S. R. (1989). *The 7 Habits of Highly Effective People.* Free Press.
- Crouse, K. (2019). *Serving Herself: The Life and Times of Serena Williams.* Farrar, Straus and Giroux.

D
- Davis, B. O. (1991). *Benjamin O. Davis, Jr.: American.* Smithsonian Institution Press.
- DeFrantz, T. F. (2004). *Dancing Revelations: Alvin Ailey's Embodiment of African American Culture.* Oxford University Press.
- Descharnes, R., & Néret, G. (2001). *Salvador Dalí: The Paintings.* Taschen.
- Duckworth, A. (2016). *Grit: The Power of Passion and Perseverance.* Scribner.

- DuVernay, A. (Director). (2014). *Selma* [Film]. Paramount Pictures.
- DuVernay, A. (Director). (2016). *13th* [Film]. Netflix.
- Dweck, C. S. (2006). *Mindset: The New Psychology of Success.* Random House.

E
- Eilish, B., & O'Connell, F. (2019). *When We All Fall Asleep, Where Do We Go?* [Album]. Darkroom/Interscope Records.
- Elsen, A. E. (2003). *Rodin.* Museum of Modern Art.

F
- Ferriss, T. (2007). *The 4-Hour Workweek.* Crown Publishing Group.
- Fischer, L. (1982). *The Life of Mahatma Gandhi.* Harper & Row.
- Forleo, M. (2019). *Everything Is Figureoutable.* Portfolio.
- Fraser, L. (2000). *J.K. Rowling: The Wizard Behind Harry Potter.* Wiley.

G
- Gabler, N. (2019). *Beyoncé: The Making of a Pop Icon.* HarperCollins.
- Gardner, H. (1983). *Frames of Mind: The Theory of Multiple Intelligences.* Basic Books.
- Gardner, H. (1993). *Multiple Intelligences: The Theory in Practice.*
  Basic Books.
- Gates, M. F. (2022). *The Moment of Lift: How Empowering Women Changes the World.* Flatiron Books.
- Gehry, F. (2009). *The Complete Works.* Taschen.
- Gjerde, M. (2003). *Jack LaLanne: Revolutionary Fitness Legend.* Fitness Press.
- Goleman, D. (1995). *Emotional Intelligence: Why It Can Matter More Than IQ.* Bantam Books.
- Goleman, D. (2006). *Emotional Intelligence: Why It Can Matter More Than IQ.* Bantam.
- Griswold del Castillo, R., & Garcia, R. (1995). Cesar Chavez: A Triumph of Spirit. University of Oklahoma Press.

H

- Haber, L. (1991). *Black Pioneers of Science and Invention.* Harcourt.
- Hamilton, A. (2020). *It's About Damn Time: How to Turn Being Underestimated into Your Greatest Advantage.* Currency.
- Harris, A. (2021). *Denzel Washington: A Biography.* Greenwood.
- Hauser, T. (1991). *Muhammad Ali: His Life and Times.* Simon & Schuster.
- Heller, S., & Scher, P. (2008). *Make It Bigger.* Princeton Architectural Press.
- Herrera, H. (2002). *Frida: A Biography of Frida Kahlo.* Harper Perennial.
- Hitchcock, A., & Truffaut, F. (1984). *Hitchcock.* Simon & Schuster.
- Hoghe, R. (2008). *Pina Bausch: Dance Theater.* Editions L'Arche.
- Huerta, D. (2008). *Dolores Huerta: A Hero to Migrant Workers.* HarperCollins.
- Huxtable, A. L. (2004). *Frank Lloyd Wright: A Life.* Penguin Books.

I

- Isaacson, W. (2007). *Einstein: His Life and Universe.* Simon & Schuster.
- Isaacson, W. (2011). *Steve Jobs.* Simon & Schuster.
- Isherwood, C. (2015, August 6). Review: *'Hamilton,' Young Rebels Changing History and Theater. The New York Times.*
- Itzkoff, D. (2018). *Robin.* Henry Holt and Co.

J

- Jacobs, J. (1961). *The Death and Life of Great American Cities.* Random House.
- John, D., & Paisner, D. (2007). *Display of Power: How FUBU Changed a World of Fashion, Branding and Lifestyle.* Naked Ink.
- Jodidio, P. (2009). *Architecture Now! Frank Gehry.* Taschen.

K

- Kean, T. H., & Hamilton, L. H. (2004). *The 9/11 Commission Report: Final Report of the National Commission on Terrorist Attacks Upon the United States*. W. W. Norton & Company.
- Keegan, R. (2009). *James Cameron: Interviews*. University Press of Mississippi.
- Kelley, K. (2010). *Oprah: A Biography*. Crown Archetype.
- Kent, S. (2001). *The Ultimate History of Video Games*. Three Rivers Press.
- King, M. L. (2018). *The Good Neighbor: The Life and Work of Fred Rogers*. Abrams Press.
- Kirkpatrick, D. (2010). *The Facebook Effect: The Inside Story of the Company That Is Connecting the World*. Simon & Schuster.
- Knight, L. W. (2005). C*itizen: Jane Addams and the Struggle for Democracy*. University of Chicago Press.
- Kremer, G. R. (2011). *George Washington Carver: In His Own Words, Second Edition*. University of Missouri Press.

L

- Lashinsky, A. (2012). *Inside Apple: How America's Most Admired, and Secretive, Company Really Works*. Business Plus.
- Lash, J. P. (1980). *Helen and Teacher: The Story of Helen Keller and Anne Sullivan Macy*. Delacorte Press.
- Lazenby, R. (2014). *Michael Jordan: The Life*. Little, Brown and Company.
- Layden, T. (2016). *Usain Bolt: The Fastest Man Alive*. Sports Illustrated Books.
- Leibovitz, A. (2008). *At Work*. Random House.
- Lemke, K. (1994). *Mary T. Washington Wylie: America's First Black Woman CPA*. NABA Publishing.
- Lemke, K. (1994). *Mary T. Washington Wylie: America's First Black Woman CPA*. NABA Publishing.

M

- Ma, Y. (2018). *Beginner's Mind.* Harvard University Lecture Series.
- Maathai, W. (2006). *Unbowed: A Memoir.* Knopf.
- Madsen, A. (1990). *Chanel: A Woman of Her Own.* Henry Holt.
- Mandela, N. (1995). *Long Walk to Freedom: The Autobiography of Nelson Mandela.* Little, Brown and Company.
- Marán, R. (2010). *Clemente: The Passion and Grace of Baseball's Last Hero.* Touchstone.
- McCullough, D. (1972). *The Great Bridge: The Epic Story of the Building of the Brooklyn Bridge.* Simon & Schuster.
- Meisler, A. (2021). S*atya Nadella: The Reimagining of Microsoft.*
  Harper Business.
- Miranda, L. M. (2015). *Hamilton: An American Musical* [Stage performance].
- Montgomery, R. (2002). *Nikola Tesla: Inventor of the Electrical Age.* Wiley.
- Montessori, M. (1964). *The Montessori Method.* Schocken Books.
- Morris, B. J. (2003). M*aggie Lena Walker and the Independent Order of*
  St. Luke. University of Virginia Press.
- Munroe, A. (2012). *Yayoi Kusama: Infinity Mirrors.* Hirshhorn Museum.

N

- Naifeh, S., & Smith, G. W. (2011). *Van Gogh: The Life.* Random House.
- Nooyi, I. (2021). *My Life in Full: Work, Family, and Our Future.* Portfolio.

O

- Obama, B. (2006). *The Audacity of Hope: Thoughts on Reclaiming the American Dream.* Crown.
- Ogilvy, D. (1985). *Ogilvy on Advertising.* Crown Publishing.

P

- Parks, G. (1966). *A Choice of Weapons.* Viking Press.
- Passman, D. S. (2015). *All You Need to Know About the Music Business (9th ed.).* Simon & Schuster.
- Perkins, M. (2021). *The Canva Story. Canva Blog.* https://www.canva.com/newsroom/
- Petroski, H. (2006). *The Essential Engineer: Why Science Alone Will Not Solve Our Global Problems.* Knopf.
- Pierson, R. (2013). *Every child needs a champion* [TED Talk]. https://www.ted.com

R

- Ramsay, G. (2006). *Gordon Ramsay's Fast Food.* HarperCollins.
- Ratey, J. J., & Hagerman, E. (2008). Spark: *The Revolutionary New Science of Exercise and the Brain.* Little, Brown.
- Richardson, J. (1991). *A Life of Picasso: Volume I.* Random House.
- Robinson, T. (2014). *Christopher Nolan: A Critical Study of the Films.* McFarland.
- Rogers, C. R. (1961). *On Becoming a Person: A Therapist's View of Psychotherapy.* Houghton Mifflin.
- Rogers, N. A. (2013). *Charles Drew: Doctor Who Got the World Pumped Up to Give Blood.* Enslow Publishers.
- Rubin, J. (2002). *Haruki Murakami and the Music of Words.* Harvill Press.
- Runco, M. A., & Jaeger, G. J. (2012). The standard definition of creativity. *Creativity Research Journal, 24(1),* 92–96. https://doi.org/10.1080/10400419.2012.650092

S

- Sandberg, S. (2013). *Lean In: Women, Work, and the Will to Lead.* Knopf.
- Saward, J. (2005). *The Grand Prix Saboteurs.* Motorbooks.
- Schmidt, E., & Rosenberg, J. (2014). *How Google Works.* Grand Central Publishing.
- Schultz, H., & Yang, D. J. (2011). *Onward: How Starbucks Fought for Its Life Without Losing Its Soul.* Rodale.

- Scobie, C. (2016). *Adele: The Biography.* HarperCollins.
- Shetterly, M. L. (2016). *Hidden Figures: The American Dream and the Untold Story of the Black Women Mathematicians Who Helped Win the Space Race.* William Morrow.
- Shpigel, B. (2020, February 18). *Simone Biles Is the Best Gymnast Ever. The New York Times.* https://nytimes.com
- Smith, M. (2016). *Netflix and the Culture of Reinvention.* Harvard Business Review Press.
- Smith, S. (2013). *J.K. Rowling: A Biography – The Genius Behind Harry Potter.* Greenwood.
- Sotomayor, S. (2013). *My Beloved World.* Vintage.
- Stand and Deliver. (1988). [Film]. Warner Bros.
- Stein, D. (1985). Ada: *A Life and Legacy.* MIT Press.
- Stone, B. (2013). *The Everything Store: Jeff Bezos and the Age of Amazon.* Little, Brown.

T
- Thomas, V. (1985). *Partners of the Heart.* University of Pennsylvania Press.
- Toffler, A. (1970). *Future Shock.* Random House.
- Tutu, D. (2011). *God Is Not a Christian: And Other Provocations.* HarperOne.

U
- U.S. Department of Energy. (2016). *Frederick McKinley Jones:* A Cooling Pioneer. https://energy.gov

V
- Vance, A. (2015). *Elon Musk: Tesla, SpaceX, and the Quest for a Fantastic Future.* HarperCollins.
- Verducci, T. (2014). *The Captain: The Journey of Derek Jeter.* Penguin Press.

W
- Watts, S. (2005). *The People's Tycoon: Henry Ford and the American Century.* Knopf.
- Winfrey, O. (1998). *The Uncommon Wisdom of Oprah Winfrey: A Portrait in Her Own Words.* Carol Publishing Group.

- Windhorst, B. (2020). LeBron, Inc.: *The Making of a Billion-Dollar Athlete.*
  St. Martin's Press.

Y
- Yousafzai, M., & Lamb, C. (2013). *I Am Malala: The Girl Who Stood Up for Education and Was Shot by the Taliban.* Little, Brown and Company.

Z
- Zardini, M. (2000). *Zaha Hadid: The Complete Buildings and Projects.* Rizzoli.

Share the Wisdom. Spread the Genius.

If Unlocking Your Natural Genius sparked something in you; clarity, confidence, or a deeper sense of purpose, don't keep it to yourself.

- Share this book with a friend, colleague, or student who needs encouragement on their journey.
- If you found value in these pages, we'd love to hear from you!

Leave a quick review on Google and let others know how this book impacted you.